THE ART OF COARSE RUGBY

D0921420

Also in Arrow Books by Michael Green

The Art of Coarse Drinking
The Art of Coarse Acting
The Art of Coarse Golf
The Art of Coarse Sailing
The Art of Coarse Moving
The Art of Coarse Sport

Michael Green

THE ART OF COARSE
RUGBY

or

Any Number Can Play

Illustrated by
JOHN JENSEN

ARROW BOOKS

Arrow Books Ltd
3 Fitzroy Square, London W1

An imprint of the Hutchinson Publishing Group

London Melbourne Sydney Auckland
Wellington Johannesburg and agencies
throughout the world

First published by Hutchinson & Co (Publishers) Ltd 1960
Arrow edition (revised and reset) 1967
Second impression 1969
Third impression 1970
Fourth impression 1973
Fifth impression 1976
Sixth impression 1977
Revised edition © Michael Green 1967

Made and printed in Great Britain
by The Anchor Press Ltd
Tiptree, Essex

ISBN 0 09 908530 5

Introduction to the Paperback Edition

I wrote *Coarse Rugby* in 1960 and it was based largely on my experiences in the postwar period and the fifties. Since then the game has changed and like so much else has been affected by the social revolution of the sixties. References to teams playing under primitive conditions may seem rather dated now that so many clubs have built new pavilions and improved their grounds. There aren't many sides these days who carry their posts to the park and change in an old garage (although a few still do that sort of thing, I'm glad to say). References to players biting each other, which might have been hilarious at the time of writing, have an unpleasant association now first-class players have started doing it. The traditional high spirits of the rugby player on tour threatened to get out of hand and hotel-wrecking is no longer considered amusing. Some of the diagrams even refer to the old 3–2–3 scrum formation which younger players will not remember.

In revising the book for the paperback edition I considered whether to correct all these anomalies but in the end I decided against it. In several places I have amended the text, sometimes for literary reasons, but in general it was impossible to alter the book too much without destroying its spirit. So I decided to let it stand much as it was originally, and if any parts of it seem out of date let it be considered as an historical record and a tribute to all the gallant Coarse Rugby heroes of the past who kept the game going without the aid of plate-glass pavilions and fruit machines.

Fortunately, the true spirit of Coarse Rugby is far from dead, despite the greater sophistication of the game today. Recently I revisited my old club in Leicester, now resplendent in a smart new pavilion. It seemed a far cry from the old days until a friend rushed up and said, 'You ought to have been with us last week, Mike. We left Leicester with fourteen men, lost two on the way, picked up a complete stranger in the car park and won 10-nil with thirteen players.'

Somehow, somewhere, Coarse Rugby will always flourish. Long may it continue to do so.

MICHAEL GREEN

London 1967

Foreword

BY SPIKE HUGHES

London Irish and Austria

Nobody need think that because I once wrote a book on *The Art of Coarse Cricket* I have no qualifications to write an introduction to this book on *The Art of Coarse Rugby*. There are—though I say it—few better qualified to do so than myself, for I can claim the rare distinction of having played in a Coarse Rugby *international*. This memorable occasion took place many years ago and began late one night in the bar of a Viennese night club called the Moulin Rouge. I was sitting there, quietly minding my own business, when a young Englishman from our Legation pleaded with me to play rugby the following afternoon. They were playing the Rumanians, he explained. Who were 'They'? I asked. Austria, I was told. At least, they supposed it was Austria. It was the only side in the country and they were playing the only side in Rumania. I protested that I didn't understand why I should be selected for such an important match. I wasn't being 'selected', I was told, I was being invited, if not actually begged, to play. A group of South African medical students and one or two members of the British Legation in Vienna had committed themselves (I have never discovered how or why) to play the Rumanians three times in three days. It was a considerable journey from Bucharest to Vienna and it hadn't been thought worth while to play just one international rugby match: there had to be three. Two of the games had already been played, the casualty list—on the Austrian side, at least —had been enormous, and as the final match would decide the rubber, recruits of any class were desperately needed. I accepted.

The match was played in a large local soccer stadium capable of holding 30,000 spectators, but on this occasion entirely empty but for the groundsman's small son who was persuaded to retrieve the ball for us whenever it was kicked into one of the stands. There was a great deal of kicking as far into the stands as possible. We were all in sore need of every possible moment of respite and it was quickly impressed on the boy that it would do his father's carefully tended pitch irreparable harm if he rode his bicycle across it from one touch-line to the other. He must go round the ground to fetch the ball —and 'round the ground' meant by way of the dead ball line. The average time taken between the kick to touch and the subsequent line-out was two extremely welcome minutes. It was an admirable arrangement, satisfactory to both sides. By some form of bush telegraph the result —Rumania 15 points, Austria 9 points—appeared under the heading 'Ruggby Fussball' in the sports pages of the following morning's papers which I read in bed, where I stayed, crippled by stiffness, for the next week.

The point of this personal reminiscence is to demonstrate that anybody who writes a book about Coarse Rugby must expect the same treatment from his readers as the author of a book on Coarse Cricket. He will be read with enjoyment and tears of laughter will run down his readers' cheeks, but when they have read the book they will put it down and say, in a smug and patronising way, that yes, it's very nice, but really nothing compared with the time when they played—well, for Austria against Rumania, for instance. Michael Green will be considered to have understated preposterously by those who know what he is talking about and to have exaggerated beyond the bounds of decency by those who don't. He needn't worry, for he knows—and so, by the scrum-cap of the Prophet, does the Rugby Union—that he and his kind are the very blood and backbone of the Handling Code (I worked on the sports desk of the *Daily Herald* one afternoon during the war). Without them, not only would thousands more of us be able to get tickets for Twickenham, but the world of Coarse Cricket would slowly grind to a deathly standstill. More true Coarse Cricketers have been recruited from the ranks of the Extra Bs and Extra Cs than from any other section of society, for they have in unique measure the indifference to physical discomfort and climatic conditions, the unswerving sense of purpose, the lack of skill, the cunningly concealed ability to observe the letter, without for one moment observing the spirit, of the laws proclaimed from the Mosaic heights of Lord's and Twickenham, and above all the sense of humour without which sport of any kind can become a crashing bore of Olympic proportions.

Those of us who have, on the whole, preferred to pass our winter Saturday afternoons in front of a fire, have never ceased to marvel at the devotion of those anonymous stalwarts of the Extra Bs, splashing around in six inches of mud and miles from the nearest railway station, who are the heroes of Michael Green's moving and hilarious book. The reader, however, must not expect to learn what it is that impels thousands of otherwise normal young men throughout the British Isles to spend their spare time in this way. Neither Mr. Green nor anybody else will ever be able to explain that, because—in the words of the grandfather of a famous England cricket captain:

> 'Theirs not to reason why,
> Theirs but to do or die . . .'

Few words (except perhaps the whole of the rest of that poem) can express more clearly the dauntless spirit of those who practise, love and respect the Art of Coarse Rugby.

Preface

I do not wish to pay the author's customary tribute to his old college tutor for correcting the proofs of the book, because I have no old college tutor (in fact I haven't even got an old college), and even if I had, I would not have allowed him to touch the proofs. Neither do I wish to praise the devotion of my wife for typing the manuscript, for the same reason. But I would like to thank the kind friends who have helped to provide material, either knowingly or unknowingly. I hope that some of them may even remain my friends, although I can see no reason why they should. I am also grateful to the many clubs with which I have been associated. However, where I refer to a club under a fictitious name, no sinister reference is intended to any particular team and such names represent types of club rather than individual sides.

A small part of the material in the book originally appeared in *The Observer* in my two

articles 'Gentlemen Will Please Refrain' and
'Extraordinary Extra B'.

Finally, I must take this unique opportunity
of raising the traditional fingers of scorn at the
man who deliberately kicked me in the back
when I fell on the ball while playing in Hert-
fordshire some years ago. I have always wished
to insult him.

I

'Well there I was with the line in front of me, and I thought to myself how daft to risk dribbling the ball with the foot, so I simply picked up the thing and ran over the line and touched down. I didn't half get a wigging from our skipper, I can tell you, and as for the Head, he was furious.'—William Webb Ellis, traditionally the originator of modern rugger, 1823 (dub.).

Anyone who plays rugby very soon finds out there are two sorts. The first kind of rugby is called rugger. Rugger is played by fifteen men on each side. These fifteen men are devoted enthusiasts who train like mad. They don't mind at all if someone tackles them at thirty miles an hour and sends them flying into the grandstand, they merely grin and tousle their opponent's hair playfully.

If they are injured, rugger players are very brave. They pretend it is nothing really and as soon as they are able to stand they hobble back into play and everyone claps them, especially the other side.

After the game rugger players all declare

what fine fellows their opponents are, and they all cheer and clap each other on the back, and sometimes exchange jerseys. Both teams then wallow in a luxurious hot bath, eat an enormous tea, and indulge in great *bonhomie* together in the evening.

Rugger is controlled by an International Board who issue edicts about open play and the Spirit of the Game. In turn, the board is composed of representatives of the various Unions who send round men to speak at club dinners and to exhort everyone to follow the Spirit of the Game. This includes being celibate on Friday night.

Games of rugger are controlled by a referee and two touch-judges. The referee's decision is final and even if a player disagrees with it he doesn't show it, but grins and bears it in the Spirit of the Game.

Unfortunately, half the rugby played in this country bears little resemblance to the splendid conception fostered by the Rugby Union. The 'other half' consists of the third, fourth, fifth and sixth teams of the less-fashionable clubs, or the first and second XVs of the very small clubs. This submerged section of the rugby world play Coarse Rugby. The rest play rugger.

The first thing that distinguishes Coarse

Rugby from rugger is that neither side is *ever* composed of fifteen men. In fact, most Extra Bs or Cs wouldn't know what to do with fifteen players. They would have to send three or four off the field before they could begin.

An old friend, a converted soccer man who played for one of the coarsest sides in the country, claimed that he was twenty-eight before he realised there was supposed to be fifteen on each side. When they told him he thought for a moment and said: 'Well, I think fifteen a side spoils it.'

What a man! His type are the very salt of Coarse Rugby.

The reason why the lower sides never have fifteen men is because they are at the mercy of the selection committee. Many of the people picked for the junior sides are just names—the bodies belonging to the names haven't been seen since they put up the subscription. Sometimes even the pretence of putting down fifteen names is dropped, and they put down ten for the Extra C and hope the other side will be just as short.

As players drop out during the week the gaps are filled from below. The third team may only be one man short, but by the time the Extra C is reached, they are lucky if they have six

players left. I don't know if any readers have
ever played six-a-side rugby. It's a jolly little
romp, but a trifle exhausting. Rather like trying
to round up a gang of wild ponies single-
handed on Bodmin Moor. Five minutes each
way is enough.

To make things worse, all six players may be
front-row forwards. Coarse Rugby men are
rarely allowed to play in their own positions.
They are simply pushed in anywhere. In fact
most of them have forgotten what their original
position was, they just describe themselves
vaguely as backs or forwards. This can make
for some interesting situations. A back division
composed entirely of hookers is not to be
sneezed at.

If a player is branded as coarse there is no
escape, no matter what he achieves. I sat on the
committee of a club for years, and still couldn't
rise past the third team. Perhaps I should have
done what someone else did, and he married
the chairman's daughter (just before the season
started). At the selection committee the chairman would say: 'Gentlemen, I shall now retire
while you discuss my son-in-law.' What could
we do?

He was selected until he was almost middle-
aged and then his wife stopped his playing,

otherwise he would still be there today.

If there is going to be a mix-up in the organisation, be sure that the coarse teams will be the chief sufferers. The fixture list from the B XV downwards is always full of vague gaps which are optimistically filled at the last moment, and not always very efficiently, as when a team drove into a ground in the East Midlands and saw another coach following them in. It turned out to be a further team of would-be opponents.

There was a somewhat acrimonious discussion between the home club and the two visiting teams as to who should play. The hosts obviously preferred to play the second side (I don't blame them, we were a dirty lot at that time). However, being first, we insisted on playing and won 40-nil as anticipated. The spare team vanished. I believe they took their coach on a gigantic pub-crawl.

Of course, occasionally these mix-ups work on behalf of the coarse team. When the committee picked sixteen for the Extra B, thinking someone was bound to drop out, they all turned up. The game had been going on for five minutes before we noticed something odd about the pack and investigation showed there were nine forwards.

We didn't tell our opponents, the skipper just asked our winger to slide quietly off the field and hide behind the hedge. By half-time he was tired of crouching there and wanted to return, so we sent someone else behind the hedge and let him come back. Not surprisingly we won 55-nil.

The captain of the other side said afterwards he was completely baffled by the clever switching of positions.

This is typical of the fine spirit in which Coarse Rugby is played. If it had been a rugger match some fool would have piped up to the referee, 'Oh, I say, sir, we're frightfully sorry, we've got sixteen men.' As it was, a good time was had by all and our opponents were none the wiser. They would have lost anyway.

But having sixteen is the exception. More often than not the Extra B are lucky to have twelve. If they want any more men they must forage for themselves. During an unbeaten run we had to seek out our own players to sustain the record. Our winger, an Australian, took us down to an underground Australian den in Fulham and recruited three shaven-headed individuals simply by shouting through the tobacco smoke, 'Would any of you jokers like a game of football next Saturday?'

We didn't really expect them to turn up, but to our surprise one of them came along and showed himself absolutely out of our class. He scored five tries and everyone slapped him on the back and said what a good fellow he was.

'Naw,' he said modestly, 'I enjoyed it. Playing thirteen-a-side was just like Rugby League back home.'

He looked in his boot afterwards and seemed disappointed at not finding anything.

It was explained gently that we were all liable to be expelled by the Rugby Union for playing with him, and he took it very well. He played several more games, but it was always a risk, because Rugby League was stamped all over his style of play (his way of playing the ball after a tackle was fascinating) and suspicions were aroused among our opponents. So it was rather a relief when he returned to Australia, leaving behind a trail of broken female hearts and an old London taxi.

Not only does Coarse Rugby have fewer players than rugby, but they are *different*. I don't mean they have three arms or two heads, although I knew a one-armed player who was very good. I mean they are a different class of person.

Rugger is a game for the fit, the enthusiastic, the young men with energy to burn. Coarse

Rugby is played by those who are too old, too young, too light, too heavy, too weak, too lazy, too slow, too cowardly or too unfit for ordinary rugger.

It is only in the coarse section of the game that a player can leave the field to rest after a try. If it happened in rugger there would be an uproar. It's nothing unusual in Coarse Rugby. We had a centre who always had to lie down on the touchline for ten minutes after a long run. When one reaches forty, you have to be careful.

While the average First XV will contain a fair sprinkling of physical training instructors, athletes and keep-fit maniacs, the Extra B will be composed mainly of seedy commercial travellers, round-shouldered clerks and gangling teenagers who have outgrown their strength. The chart opposite will show the difference between a rugger side and a coarse team. (The rugger team first.)

These are only a sample, but they are fairly typical. The soccer converts can always be identified because they hold the ball crossways when punting. It is no use telling them they ought to hold it longwise, because they always manage to kick it further and more accurately their way.

Playing in a match with several people like

RICHEATH PARK First XV

Position	Age	Weight	Height	Notes
Front-row forward	25	16 st.	5 ft. 11 in.	Solid bone and muscle. Impervious to pain.
Wing forward	22	14 st.	6 ft. 4 in.	Afraid of man nor beast. Metropolitan Police heavyweight boxing champion. Judo expert.
Stand-off	25	11 st.	5 ft. 9 in.	P.T. Instructor. Capped three times for Wales.
Wing-threequarter	19	11 st.	5 ft. 10 in.	County sprint champion. Runs five miles before breakfast every day. Drinks shandy.

BAGFORD VIPERS Fourth XV

Position	Age	Weight	Height	Notes
Front-row forward	46	16 st.	5 ft. 5 in.	All fat. A coward
Wing forward	17	9 st.	6 ft. 2 in.	Mother doesn't think he is strong enough to play. She is right. He, too, is yellow.
Stand-off	48	11 st.	5 ft. 9 in.	Still has five German bullets in his leg, which slow him down Father of seven.
Wing-threequarter	23	10 st.	5 ft. 1 in.	They got him from the local soccer team and he doesn't know the rules yet.

this is a fascinating experience. If tackled they sometimes become very annoyed and try to appeal to the referee. They settle down pretty quickly in the scrum, but they completely lose their heads when they find themselves with the ball in the open.

One ex-centre-half fought through the ruck and then generously threw the ball twenty yards forward to me, with a cry of 'Here you are mate, have a go yourself.' He was obviously so delighted at his success that I didn't like to disillusion him, so I ran like mad and pretended to be disappointed when the whistle blew for a forward pass.

A comparison between rugger and Coarse Rugby players also shows some interesting contrasts in the reasons why people play the game. The rugger man plays because he enjoys it. The Coarse Rugby man plays for almost every other reason.

He may play because he likes the company: to get away from his wife; to keep fit; because he's bullied into it; because he hopes one day to play in the first team; because he's learning the game; because father played; because he hopes it will make a man of him; or because he daren't admit he's too old. Of course he may enjoy the game as well, if it's a nice afternoon and his side win.

Because the men who play it are different, Coarse Rugby has none of that phoney stuff about not caring if someone tackles you. Coarse Rugby players *resent* being dragged into the mud. At their age the consequences could be fatal.

No, as Dr. Johnson said, you must 'clear your mind of cant' when playing Coarse Rugby. If you subject an Extra B player to a real Twickenham flying tackle he will probably get up and kick you. And serve you right, too. There is a refreshing candour about the coarse game, with none of this 'Think nothing of it old man' attitude if you get hurt.

The first thing a coarse player does on re-gaining his senses after an injury is to shout, 'Let me get at the dirty rat.' If he is lucky, his colleagues will add loudly, 'Don't worry, Joe, we'll fix him at the next line-out.'

I was once nearly injured myself as a result of mistaken identity in one of these vendettas. I was running along, minding my own busi-ness, nowhere near the ball, when someone tripped me up from behind and trod on the back of my neck. After recovering I sought out the smallest and weakest man on the other side and did the same to him. Finally everyone was doing it and the ball was forgotten.

It was only after the game that we found out my assailant had mistaken me for a player who had injured his brother in the previous season.

After that we were all good friends, although we let down his car tyres when we left, just to show he wasn't forgotten.

Coarse Rugby is also free from one of the fallacies that has plagued rugger (and cricket too, for that matter) for years. This is the myth that an invisible Union Jack flies over every scrum, that rugby is a preparation for the Greater Game of Life. Speaking for myself, I think it would be most inconvenient if a Union Jack flew over every scrum. Perhaps that is what was wrong with the England pack a few years ago.

This myth is chiefly perpetuated by certain writers of rugby verse who turn out stuff like this (I give an imaginary example written by myself):

> With *ungirt loins I face the foe,
> Their clutching hands elude.
> I hear not all the players' cries,
> Their honest voices †rude.

* Strictly this means he hasn't got any trousers on, but that is not the meaning here. All the poets use this phrase. Loins—which is not a misprint for lions by the way—is not a word which is quite drawing-room conversation, but as it's poetry anything goes.

† 'Rude' as used here, does not mean everyone was going round shouting obscene words, it means their voices were a little rough.

My feet scarce touch the muddy earth
As o'er the *sward I fly.
The line is 'neath my pounding boots,
I dive—I've scored a try.

And thus it is in life itself,
In life as in Rugby's game.
†Ungird your loins, my boy, and strive
For the goal of an honest name.

The people who write this sort of thing cannot leave rugby simply as a game. Behind
every threequarter move they see the helio-
graph flicker over the hills, where a young
officer in a sun helmet three sizes too big for
him is talking through clenched teeth to his
men (all soccer types, but good fellers with the
right leader).

Every line-out becomes a miniature Omdur-
man, every scrum a second Ladysmith.

Well, this is a very fine thought but in prac-

* 'Sward' is not one of those things the knights used
to carve each other up with, but is a poetic word for
grass. Come to think of it, I might as well have said
'grass'.

† Again, strictly this means, 'Take off your trousers, my
boy,' but that is not what I mean. After all, you can't
have people exposing themselves all over rugby pitches,
can you? No, it is just poetic language for 'Get stuck in,
lad'.

tice we all know that rugger heroes have just as many human feelings as anyone else. The golden-haired boy inspiring his side to victory may be trying to get out of his National Service. Hands up all rugger players who have ever missed a draft because they were needed for a big game. Thank you.

Fortunately, Coarse Rugby is spared this myth because no one in his right senses could conceive of the game imparting any special characteristics except juvenile delinquency.

One of the most certain ways of distinguishing a Coarse Rugby game—other than by counting the players—is to look at the ball. Coarse Rugby is played with a repulsive, rhomboidal object that is a cross between a rugger ball and a soccer ball. On the whole it is more like a soccer ball. It is certainly more round than oblong and bears little relation to those white, torpedo-like things they use at Twickenham. Accurate kicking with it is impossible.

Besides being nearly round it is twice as heavy as a proper rugger ball, and it is black. It is a mystery as to how Coarse Rugby balls become round and black and heavy. I used to think that they were like that when new, but they apparently start off as ordinary balls and become like that. Perhaps they are re-moulds.

The ball is also traditionally under-inflated. If both sides are pressed hard they will meet. The stitching on the seams is usually coming undone, although this can be turned to advantage.

Back home in the Midlands a certain third team player used to hold the ball by a piece of thread from the seam and do all sorts of things with it. The ball apparently stuck to his palm, and he made the most wonderful dummies. The other side waited for him to drop the ball but he never did, of course.

Eventually he used to work the seam loose before the game and run along bouncing the ball like a yo-yo. But that was overdoing it, even for us. Besides, all the balls started to fall apart.

Another distinguishing mark of Coarse Rugby is the amount of noise. The lower down the rugby scale one goes, the greater the din.

Internationals are carried on—as far as the players are concerned—in grim silence, broken only by the snapping of an odd bone or the crunch of someone's skull giving way.

Coarse Rugby games are played in a babble of sound. There are frenzied shouts of advice, cries of encouragement, bellowed insults and just general chatter about the weather.

The amount of advice one receives is astonishing. No sooner have you received a pass than six people start shouting what to do with the ball. They never remotely agree. Some want you to run, others to kick and the rest urge you to get rid of it. Not that they know anything about it. Hulking forwards who have never scored a try in their lives will boom detailed instructions on how to perform a scissors movement. The voice of the captain is drowned or ignored. A howl of execration marks the inevitable tackle.

For some reason, Old Boys' teams are more vocal than anyone. They seem to breed a demagogue-type pack-leader with a high-pitched, piercing voice, who does no work at all except to run round the field squawking madly in a frightfully suburban accent.

'Oh do come on Old Rottinghamians,' he shrieks. 'You really must stop them breaking through like that. Hold him, Old Rotts . . . hold him. That's better. No, no, don't let him go, hold him. Now then, Old Rotts, all together and let's tear into them. No, no, no, Old Rotts, we want to heel, not take.'

These pack-leaders never stop talking, even when injured, but continue to gasp exhortations while lying prone on the touch-line.

The absence of touch-judges adds another air of glorious uncertainty to Coarse Rugby. This is often increased by the absence of proper touch-lines and by the lack of a referee as well. The absence of a referee need not, however, hold up play. I have had some interesting games in which everything has been decided by general consent. Mind you, nobody scored.

Every time a player crossed the line, the defending captain would say he thought there had been a forward pass and there would be a scrum back. The other side put over a drop goal once but our skipper quickly shouted, 'Not in straight', and started to get the scrum down again. This caused a slight hiatus because the opposition had already marched back to half-way for the re-start while our forwards were forming a scrum by themselves on the 25. It took some time to sort that lot out.

As the pitches reserved for Coarse Rugby are usually remote stretches of untended sod, covered in stones, the lack of well-defined lines can be entertaining. During a fog players have been known to touch down on a neighbouring hockey pitch, and the occasional loose maul filtered over too, to the consternation of the women playing there.

But all this is in the best tradition of the early

rugby pioneers. They didn't have clearly-defined lines at Rugby in Tom Brown's day and they didn't have a referee either. In fact, a close examination of Chapter Five of *Tom Brown's Schooldays* reveals that in Tom Brown's historic match one side had 120 players and the other sixty.

And that is a typical Coarse Rugby situation if ever there was one.

2

'That we may wander o'er this bloody field . . .'—
> Shakespeare (Henry V).

It is a wet, drizzling, bitterly cold Saturday afternoon in February. A group of dismal figures in motley rugby kit are shambling along a rough cinder path between a refuse dump and a field of thistles. Behind them a coach driver who unwisely tried to drive down the path is endeavouring to extricate his vehicle from the ditch.

A player at the back of the group speaks. He is a tall lanky man in his late thirties with receding hair and a pronounced stoop. We shall call him Thinny, and he is the Old Rottinghamians Extra B stand-off. He furtively adjusts his surgical underwear as he speaks.

THINNY: Gosh it's cold. Why the hell does the Extra B pitch have to be so far from the pavilion? I don't know why we play the stupid game. You wouldn't think it was February would you? More like December.

Nobody replies. They trudge moodily along in silence. Thinny tries again.

THINNY (*blowing into cupped hands*): I said I thought it was too cold to play.

This at last rouses some response in his companion, a gross, waddling creature of about thirty-nine, wearing a tattered scrum cap and a faded, patched jersey. We shall call him Fatty.

FATTY: All right. We heard you. You aren't the only one. My mind may not be the delicate mechanism that yours is, but I can get just as cold as you can. To hear you go on, anyone'd think you were the only person in the world who ever got cold. It's all right for you. You don't have to keep going down in the mud like I do.

Thinny does not reply. He is too busy lighting a cigarette from the butt of another. Fatty pursues his theme.

FATTY: I don't know why we go through this stupid torture week after week. My wife and kids think I'm nuts. Why don't we sit at home and watch the telly? That's what I like about watching an international—seeing all those stupid fools running around injuring themselves and getting all uncomfortable in the rain and I'm sitting in the warm, drinking whisky and smoking myself sick.

The pair are joined by a third player, whom we shall call Gloomy. He is a lanky youth of about nine-

teen who has outgrown his strength and his mental powers.

GLOOMY: It'll be murder in this mud. You know the boiler's furred up and there won't be any water after the first team have had their bath?

Neither of his companions reply. Fatty lights up a butt end.

GLOOMY: Cor, don't the other side look huge? See that big bloke—I bet he's the wing forward. I bet when he tackles you he absolutely flattens you. You'd better watch out, Thinny.

Fatty and Thinny purse their lips and plod on in silence.

GLOOMY (*warming to his theme*): They say that bloke who broke his leg last week may have to have it off. . . .

This produces an instantaneous reaction on Fatty and Thinny, who blench and groan.

THINNY: Shut up, will ya?

GLOOMY: Must be rotten to have your leg off. Did you hear the crack when the bone snapped? I bet he wishes he never played last week. . . .

FATTY: Will you shut up if I give you a fag?

GLOOMY: Ta, very much. I knew a boy at school who died after smoking a fag just before a game. It affected his heart.

THINNY: I'll affect your heart in a minute. It's

bad enough having to turn out on a foul
afternoon like this without you making it
worse.

GLOOMY: You ought to give up if you feel like
that. You're old enough . . . you must be about
forty-five.

THINNY: That's just it—you give up now and
you admit old age. Once you stop at my age
you never start again. It's like a woman putting
on her first corset. It's an admission you're old.

GLOOMY: They say it's dangerous to play after
thirty-five. The valves of the heart won't work
properly. . . .

*He is interrupted by a clod of wet earth on the back
of the neck. The little group trudge on in silence. It is a
quarter of an hour before they reach the pitch, which is
a sodden, lumpy meadow, bearing strong evidence of
having been recently occupied by a herd of cows with
loose bowels. They are greeted by their captain, a
harassed man of about thirty, who is probably the
slowest centre threequarter in Europe.*

CAPTAIN: Come on, where do you think you've
all been? I wanted you. We've got to rearrange
the forwards somehow.

FATTY: How many men have we got?

CAPTAIN: Eleven, not counting Knocker.

FATTY: He's not coming. I saw him in the Royal
Oak and he said to tell you he was ill.

CAPTAIN (*bitterly*): The swine! And I think the others have got thirteen. That means we're two down.

THINNY (*instantly*): Cancel it. Say the ground's unfit. Look at it, it *is* unfit. I'm sinking in up to my ankles. (*Becoming feverish and hysterical*) I tell you it's unfit to play, I tell you we can't play on this. . . . I tell you it's absurd . . . aaaaaaaaaahhhhh . . . (*he breaks off in a paroxysm of coughing as his cigarette smoke goes the wrong way*).

GLOOMY: I reckon he'll burst a lung before half-time.

The referee approaches. He is an earnest man, in late middle-age, kind-hearted and slow-witted. He can never understand why he is always allocated Extra B games.

REFEREE: Come along, Old Rottinghamians. It'll be dark soon. We're nearly an hour late already.

CAPTAIN: Coming, sir. O.K. you chaps, let's get sorted out. Jack, you'll have to be a sort of wing-three and full-back in one, and Fred, you float around generally between the pack and the backs. Use your discretion. We'll pack three-two-zero.

THINNY: Who'll go centre now Knocker's ratted on us?

CAPTAIN (*desperately*): Oh, George'll have to play centre.

GEORGE (*protesting*): But I'm a hooker.

CAPTAIN: Well, you're a centre now. Come on, stop this arguing and get stuck into them, Old Rottinghamians.

He says this without much conviction, and privately whispers to those around him, 'Don't hurry too much lads, let the bastards wait.' This is because the longer the start is delayed, the less time there will be for play, which is to the Old Rottinghamians' advantage in their weakened state. In any case, play is delayed because the match ball has landed in a heap of cow dirt, and no one will wipe it clean. Eventually the unpleasant task is performed by the captain of the opposing side, who realises that as far as the Old Rottinghamians are concerned, it can stay there for ever.

Finally the opposition kick off in gathering gloom and at an hour when most first-class matches are just finishing. The ball is caught by Thinny who drops it. An opposing forward picks it up, knocks on four times and passes forward to a colleague, who puts one foot into touch and then dives over by the corner flag, dropping the ball as he does so.

The referee, who has not moved from the centre line, promptly awards a try.

OLD ROTTINGHAMIANS (*all together*): Hey ref, he went into touch! Hey, ref, what about the knock-on? Hey, ref, what about the forward pass? Hey, ref, what about the obstruction?

Fatty even goes so far as to stand ostentatiously waiting for the line-out, but the referee is adamant.

CAPTAIN (*self-righteously*): Stop moaning, Old Rottinghamians. Never mind if the ref's a short-sighted old sheep who doesn't know the rules, it doesn't help moaning.

He realises he is standing about three feet from the referee and moves hurriedly away. Fortunately, the referee is deaf as well as short-sighted, and in any case he is used to a torrent of abuse from both sides. Meanwhile about four of the Old Rottinghamians have gathered under the crossbar. Fatty, Thinny and one or two others have flung themselves on the ground panting and grumbling.

The opposition kicker is now placing the ball with infinite pains. He has so far taken four minutes over this. Eventually he carefully marches backwards for about thirty paces and stands rigidly at attention before moving forward into an immense run. This is carried out to an accompaniment of continuous sotto voce *jeering, blasphemy, insults and obscenity from the Old Rottinghamians, none of whom, however, can raise the energy to charge.*

When the kicker reaches the ball, he aims a terrific lunge and digs his toe deep into the ground about two feet in front of it, leaving it quite undisturbed. With a

*look of intense agony he sinks slowly to the ground,
clutching his shattered leg. Quick to seize this advantage, the Old Rottinghamian skipper leads his men in
a belated charge. Ignoring the ball and the objections
of the referee they trample all over the prostrate
kicker, who recovers with alarming suddenness and
fights his way clear, protesting.*

*Order is at last restored and another kick taken.
This time the ball goes bowling along the ground and
hits the corner flag. The kicker returns to the jeers of
his own team and the Old Rottinghamians prepare to
reduce the arrears.*

*It is now half-time. As the referee blows his whistle
Fatty and Thinny collapse in their tracks.*

FATTY (*coughing as if his lungs would burst, turning
red in the face and retching*):Uuuuuuuurrrrggggg-
hhhhh. Aaaahhh. Brrouge. Faaaaaaghh. Oooo-
yer . . . oooyer . . . ooyer . . . splurge . . .
bless me (*only he doesn't say 'bless'*). Gimme a
cigarette someone.

*Thinny feels in the pocket of his shorts and brings
out a filthy, bent object which might at one time have
been a cigarette. Fatty produces a book of matches
from his shorts and lights it. Then he immediately
doubles up in another paroxysm of coughing.*

THINNY (*sitting down in a deep puddle as if it was a
feather bed*): You're in a bad way, mate.

FATTY: You're telling me. Why the hell do we

go through this ghastly torture week in, week out? Saturday after Saturday the agony goes on . . . retching . . . vomiting . . . panting for breath . . . in continual pain. . . .

THINNY (*looking round hopefully*): It's getting pretty dark. With luck the ref may have to abandon it.

The captain approaches. He is a worried man. Having forgotten the lemons for the last two home games, he tied a knot in his handkerchief and remembered them. Instead, he forgot a knife and a plate, and all he can offer the two teams is two whole lemons each.

CAPTAIN: Anyone want a bit of lemon? I forgot the knife, so you'll have to try and tear a bit off.

Between them Fatty and Thinny savage the lemons into an unrecognisable pulp which is rejected contemptuously by everyone else. The other side throw their lemons over the hedge. The referee blows an optimistic chirp on his whistle. There is a faint stir among the players but no one moves. He blows again and this time one or two of the younger ones line up in some sort of order.

CAPTAIN (*making a feeble attempt to rouse his men*): Now come along, Old Rottinghamians, let's get stuck into it this half. Thirty-six-nil isn't hopeless. If they can score it, so can we. Let's get some punch and life and go . . . go . . . go. . . .

He smacks his fist into his palm with such venom that it is paralysed for the rest of the afternoon. Someone throws a bit of mud at him. Fatty discovers he has lined up with the other team and painfully crosses back to the right side.

Thinny, who is stand-off, places the ball upright for the kick-off. It falls over. With mathematical precision he carefully replaces it and stands back with the air of a master. The ball topples over again. A restive muttering grows among the forwards, who give him advice what to do with the ball. It falls over five times altogether.

Eventually Thinny lays it down sideways on the ground and takes a wild boot at it. It spins like a top and travels two feet. The second half has begun. . . .

The Old Rottinghamians' captain is hoarse with urging his men on—a job which is quite futile. But he sticks to it. 'Come on, Old Rotts,' he shouts, leading an untidy and half-hearted foot rush down the field. 'Now we've got them on the YURRRRP. . . .' This exclamation is forced from him as an opponent fly-kicks the ball with unerring accuracy straight into his navel (point first). He collapses. When he recovers the referee awards a penalty against him.

Now the score is 45-nil against the Old Rotting-hamians. Holding on to a post as they line up for a

. . . fly-kicks the ball with unerring accuracy straight into his navel (point first).

conversion, the captain tries to flog some life into them. 'Old Rottinghamians,' he bleats, 'you mustn't let them come through like that. You must mark your men. Thinny, you must tackle.'

A violent bickering ensues. Everyone turns on Gloomy, who, like a sick sheep, is forced out of the flock and retreats to the corner flag. The skipper appeals for peace.

CAPTAIN: Stop this bickering, Old Rottinghamians. We can still do it. Let's try and get just one before the end.

Nobody pays any attention to him. They are still arguing when the kick is taken. From now on their morale goes to pieces and they are solely concerned with venting their irritation somehow. The climax of this comes when Thinny, having been fairly tackled, kicks his opponent as he gets up.

OPPONENT: You rat, I'll get you for that.

THINNY: Just you make a dirty tackle like that again, and I'll fix you proper.

OPPONENT: Oh yeah?

THINNY: Yeah.

OPPONENT: Yeah?

THINNY: Yeah.

OPPONENT: Yeah?

THINNY (*snarling*): Yeah.

OPPONENT: You and who else?

THINNY: Just me.

OPPONENT: You wouldn't dare, mate.

THINNY: Wouldn't I?

OPPONENT: No.

THINNY: No?

OPPONENT: No.

Suddenly, without warning, Thinny aims a wild and amateurish swipe at his opponent which catches him harmlessly on the shoulder. He lets out a shout of rage and they rush at each other, pummelling with all their not very considerable strength.

FATTY: Go on, Thinny, show the dirty so-and-so where he gets off!

Nobody shows any signs of stopping the fight. In fact each side encourage their own man. The referee comes puffing up, blowing his whistle wildly and in vain.

REFEREE: Now then you two, come along now and stop this nonsense. This isn't how rugby men should behave.

Neither fighter pays the slightest attention. Eventually they are separated by their captains who drag them apart and hold them while they continue to wave their fists and shout at each other.

THINNY: Let me go, Fred, just let me get at that filthy hog. He's not fit to play rugby with decent people. . . .

OPPONENT: I ask you . . . was it or was it not a fair tackle? He kicked me . . . and he bit me. Look at them bite marks. I'll murder him if I get him again.

This rouses Thinny to fury and he thrashes so violently that he breaks free. This is awkward, be-

*cause he doesn't really want to fight, so he pretends to be
restrained with difficulty.*

REFEREE: Come along you two . . . shake hands
and forget it.

*After a moment's hesitation the two players advance
and take each other's hands, each of them trying to
grip the other in such a way as to hurt him. The
result is that they look like a couple of Masons en-
gaged in some remote ritual. Having failed to hurt
each other they retire muttering and the match goes on.
But not for long. It is now nearly pitch dark and lights
can be seen twinkling in nearby suburbs. The referee
looks at his watch. The first half lasted thirty-one
minutes and the second has now lasted twenty-five
minutes. It is good enough for Coarse Rugby. He
blows a long blast.*

CAPTAIN: Old Rottinghamians, three cheers
for Bagford Vipers . . . hip . . . hip . . . hooray!

*He is answered by a feeble moaning sound, so faint
that it merges with the wind which is now beginning
to whistle coldly over the pitch.*

OPPOSING CAPTAIN (*quietly*): Don't cheer them,
lads. They're the dirtiest crowd we've ever
played.

THINNY (*approaching the man he fought with a let's-
be-friends smile*): Jolly well played. Sorry we had
that little fight.

All the time he is thinking: 'Filthy swine.'

OPPONENT (*adopting a that's-all-right-I'm-big-hearted look*): Think nothing of it, mate. It was half my fault, anyway.

Secretly he is thinking: 'I hope you break your neck.'

CAPTAIN: Hey, Fatty, give me a hand with the corner posts and the other stuff.

FATTY: Get knotted. I want a fag.

There is a hurried rush to escape the chores of collecting the posts and balls and the captain dismally starts to do it himself. He is last seen lurching around in the gloom carrying four posts, three balls, a first-aid box and a duckboard, and calling feebly for aid.

The group of players walks slowly, smoking all the time, on the half-mile path to the changing rooms. It is completely dark. As they near the pavillion, the Old Rottinghamians break into a trot in an effort to reach the bath first. They know that unless they hurry the other teams will have used all the hot water and there will be only a few miserable scraps of bread and cake for tea.

Despite their hurry they are too late. The big iron bath contains only a few inches of lukewarm, muddy fluid and the teapots at table seem filled with the same liquid. Halfway through tea the Old Rottinghamians' captain arrives. He has dropped one corner post somewhere along the trail and couldn't find it.

CAPTAIN (*bitterly*): Dirty rotten lot. Leaving me

to carry everything in. I'm going to bring this up at committee. No it's no laughing matter, it's not good enough, that's the size of it. (*He whitters away to himself.*)

The bar has now opened and revolting enamel jugs are being filled with what appears to be foam. Gloomy is trying to collect half-a-crown each from Old Rottinghamians to pay for the beer. No one else will handle this job because getting blood from a stone is child's play to collecting half-a-crown for the kitty from the Old Rottinghamians' Extra B. As usual the unfortunate youth finds he is left with about four half-crowns, five promises and a couple of flat refusals (one from Thinny, who said, 'What, buy those filthy louts beer? Not me, you try someone else'). As poor Gloomy hasn't got many friends, he makes up the deficiency himself.

The flat, warm beer loosens tongues. The dismal game slides into retrospect and appears almost as a pleasant afternoon's fun. Thinny is quite cheerful as he holds forth to a group of cronies.

THINNY: As a matter of fact, I honestly think I'm fitter and faster this season. Of course, it may be imagination. It's probably simply that I'm more *experienced* now, and I know one or two little dodges such as swivelling your eyes one way and passing the other. Cliff Morgan used to do that very effectively. As a matter of

fact I got a tip from him that night we bumped
into Cardiff on the Easter tour. . . .

FATTY: Of course, if they hadn't got that try in
the first minute it might easily gone the other
way. I honestly reckon we could have won the
game with a bit more weight in the pack, I
do. . . .

*One person is out of things—the referee, who sits
dismally in a corner, sipping his beer and wondering
why everyone is ignoring him. Thinny and Fatty are
not merely ignoring him, they are shooting venomous
glances at him from time to time. He heaves a sigh.
Life is very hard for a referee in Coarse Rugby.*

*And there let us leave them all, drinking their beer,
lying to each other, vainly boasting, happy in the
thought that now they can live the fantasy—nearly
seven days separates them from the reality. In half-an-
hour they will be singing, and vowing that the opposition are all fine fellows really. Their happiness is
complete, except for one small cloud.*

*They've got to play another game before the beer
next Saturday.*

3

'I don't know what effect these men will have upon the enemy, but by God, they terrify me.'—Duke of Wellington, *after reviewing his troops.*

The object of the game of Coarse Rugby is to *win*. Let there be no mistake about that. It is fashionable to refer to the object of a sport as to have a good time and a clean open game. Nothing could be further from the thoughts of a Coarse Rugby player. He knows it is extremely doubtful if he will have a good time, as only eleven will turn up and he is not really fit enough to play these days. He prays fervently that it won't be an open game, as this means running about. And it is most unlikely to be a clean game.

No, if he can win, that is enough.

Coarse Rugby players are not alone in this attitude. Even rugger players remember best those games that were won. One does not hear first-class players saying, 'Do you remember that smashing 44-nil defeat by Cardiff?' So don't be hard on the coarse player.

It is also the object of a coarse player to win *with the least possible exertion*. Strenuous exercise can be dangerous to the average Extra B man. Besides, any fool can win by running faster and tackling harder than the opposition. It takes brains to win without over-indulging yourself physically. Anything that can be done to win without actually picking up the ball and running with it should be done. Running is a last resort.

Preparations for winning begin long before the kick-off, at the annual meeting in fact. Many a club has given its coarser teams a wonderful time by skilfully re-naming them. It is easy to take advantage of the euphemistic system of calling lower sides by letters, by which the seventh side becomes the Extra C. This system is not standardised. Some clubs call their second team the 'A', while others call it the Extra First, and the 'A' is their third team.

By juggling with the name of the second team it is possible to push all the others down a grade, e.g. the Extra B will become the C and so on. In this way the Extra B can take over some of the C's fixtures. There is no need to arrange the whole fixture list like this, just give the lads a break about once a month.

Even better is to give the lower sides names such as Undesirables or Vandals. Then nobody knows whether the Vandals are the third or the seventh team and they can be matched with anyone.

I have had some glorious games in which the third team were pitted against someone else's fifth side. We all scored tries, even the full-back, and won about 70-nil. That's my idea of a game of rugby. Not every week, perhaps, but about once a month. It makes up for all the miserable matches when it rains and you are kicked on the knee.

More preparations can be made in the week before a match, when it is customary to send the other side a card giving directions as to how to reach the ground.

This card should be as vague and misleading as possible without giving the wrong directions. This is not difficult, because coarse pitches are usually miles from anywhere. London is easily the finest place in the country for losing your opponents, and here is a typically misleading London card:

SUBURBITON R.F.C.

BY RAIL TO ACTON. TURN LEFT OUTSIDE STATION, TURN LEFT AGAIN AT TOP OF ROAD,

THEN BUS TO FIFTH TRAFFIC LIGHTS ON RIGHT,
GO DOWN ROAD BY ROW OF SHOPS (IGNORE
CRICKET GROUND SIGN), TURN SHARP LEFT BY
GROCER'S, AND GROUND IS FIFTEEN MINUTES'
WALK UP LANE AT END OF STREET.

If possible a little map should be enclosed.
Like this:

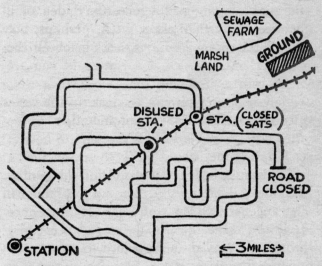

This is a beauty. The first direction, 'By rail
to Acton', should flummox them for a start, as
there are at least six stations in Acton. Even if
by some miracle they should hit the right station, no firm address is given for the ground.

They cannot ask the way to such-and-such a road. They must follow this rigmarole of leaping on and off buses and deciding which are the fifth set of traffic lights.

If they ask the way it is certain that they will receive nothing but lunatic replies. Nobody ever knows the way to a rugby pitch. The public lump all games together. Whether you ask for the rugby ground or the soccer field, you'll still be directed to the hockey pitch. The only way to find the rugby ground is to ask for the cricket ground.

Of course, if a club plays on two or three widely-separated pitches, the task is even easier. Just send no directions at all, and all the opposition will go to the First XV pitch.

Ideally, one should work these schemes so that just nine or ten opponents find the ground. If none of the other side turns up the game will be cancelled and you won't be able to win. Fortunately, there are usually enough opponents who have played there before to ensure that they don't all get lost.

Let there be no doubt as to the success of this splendid wheeze. One London suburban fourth team went through a season unbeaten simply because they changed their pitch. Good heavens, there are *still* chaps wandering around

West London trying to find the ground. If you ever meet a man carrying rugby kit and wandering aimlessly around Middlesex, just tell him the game's over will you? And tell him they lost.

This scheme can recoil on your own side, however. We lost several of our own men because of these direction cards. They joined the club and were picked for the C and were sent a direction card and we never saw them again. A pity, but they had all paid their subs so we didn't worry too much. I often wonder what became of them. One of them might have been some good. He said he used to play for Rosslyn Park.

An alternative to this scheme involves the exact opposite. Instead of trying to keep the other side from the ground, give them an embarrassing welcome. At least one London college has employed this technique with considerable effect.

When their opponents arrived all the way from Oxford they were greeted by a dozen students, and heavily plied with food and beer. Normally they would have carefully refused, but they could see the opposition tucking in, so they did the same. When the meal was over, and they were all thoroughly blown out and quite unfit to play rugby, their skipper said to one of the college men: 'How do you chaps manage to play after eating and drinking like this?'

'Oh, we don't have to play,' came the reply. 'We're just the reception committee.'

It only remains to say that the home team, who had carefully starved themselves all morning, won easily.

However, presuming you adopt the more usual course of misdirecting your opponents the next move begins as soon as they are in the changing room. At once start a war of nerves on the opposing skipper (who will be pacing up and down outside, looking for his missing players).

Let the home captain approach, pretend to look sympathetically into the distance, and then glance at his watch and start to tap his foot. Do not worry if this manœuvre has no effect for a moment. Repeat it with an occasional cough. The home team can help by coming out of the changing room and jumping up and down as if they were impatient.

Having reduced the opposing captain's nerves to shreds, remark coolly, 'I don't want to hurry you, skipper, but the ref's a bit anxious to begin. At this rate it'll be dark by half-time.

Do you think we can make a start?'

When he has no choice but to begin the game five short, produce your trump card. Offer to lend him a player.

Now I can see many veteran Coarse Rugby players rising in protest at this: 'Lend the other side a player?' they say. 'What does the man think he's doing? You should never lend the other team a man—it makes the game more even. They might even win. Anyway, you're always one or two short yourself, so why help them?'

Of course, I understand this healthy point of view, but I must emphasise that one does not lend them *any player*. Oh, dear no. One lends the player *likely to do them most harm*, which is a very different matter.

One club used to keep a special man for the purpose. In fact for years he never played for them. He always played for the opposition.

A lanky, puny, and incredibly keen youth, he was ideal for the job of unwitting sabotage. Apart from his other defects he was extremely short-sighted. But he was desperately anxious to do well. He roamed everywhere looking for the ball. Officially he was a winger, but frequently he would be found in the scrum, simply because the ball was there. Unfortunately, when

One lends the player likely to do most harm . . .

he did secure the ball, he not only didn't know what to do with it, but he was quite liable to pass to an opponent, as all the jerseys looked alike to him.

It needs little imagination to see the havoc that this one-man fifth column wrought among the opponents. No matter where they positioned him, he was so keen he would dash after the ball and then make a botch of things. Playing in the centre, he turned to take a bad pass, lost his sense of direction, and set off for his own line. The full-back just stared as he went past, touched down with a triumphant dive, and swaggered back to the centre.

No one had the heart to break the bad news to him, so they let him think he had scored, and he was as happy as a sandboy.

Good heavens, the wretched youth once touched down *on the pitch next door*. It caused much confusion over there, because there was a maul taking place near the line and at first they thought it was a genuine try and the referee whistled. Then it slowly began to dawn that this gangling adolescent was not on either side and a great argument started, until his skipper came over and gently led the lad away.

Not every team will be lucky enough to have someone so suitable, but if you find a player who promises well as a saboteur, hang on to him. He will repay you a hundredfold.

While both teams are changing, continue the attack. The period in which the opposition are undressing is of vital importance. Many a game has been lost and won then, when morale is low as players hop around on one leg looking for socks and discover in horror that they have left their boots behind. Now is the time to strike.

One of the finest dodges I know is the fake collection wheeze. In this the best actor in the side—and good acting is an essential part of Coarse Rugby—goes round the opposition with a collecting box before the game.

'I wonder if you chaps would like to contribute,' he says in a matter-of-fact tone. 'We're getting up a collection for the bloke who broke both his legs when playing against us last week. We all feel pretty upset about it I can tell you. Ginger always tackles 'em pretty hard, but he's never done anything like this before.'

Someone else should now chip in with: 'One or two people fainted when it happened. Old Ginger just dived at him at full speed and there was a great crunch, like when you tread a matchbox under your shoe. I didn't mind the way he kept twitching, it was the blood which upset me.'

As they turn pale, twist the knife in the wound. 'Actually it's a bit of a coincidence because in the same game last year one of their forwards broke eight ribs. But they say he may well partially recover.'

If you are good enough some of the opponents may even start to change back into their ordinary clothes. Incidentally, if you do collect any money, keep it to buy beer afterwards.

While they are reeling, produce another master-stroke. This is the jersey wheeze, which I have used dozens of times with the greatest success.

It was made possible because years previously I had played for Northampton second team in one game. I was reporting the match for the local paper, which I then adorned as a reporter, and Northampton were one short, so I fixed up with a colleague to report the game and offered my services.

I won't describe what happened in detail except to say that I took great exception to the man on the terrace who shouted insults simply because I failed to run fifty yards to score. I notice he never volunteered to play.

Anyway, the Saints gave me an old shirt that had been lagging a boiler pipe (it was still warm) and I kept this, although it was a little faded and charred round the edges.

When playing Coarse Rugby I used to approach the captain of the opposition, wearing this monstrosity, and say in a loud voice: 'Will this jersey clash with your colours, old man?

Actually it's a Northampton jersey. Yes, NORTHAMPTON. Northampton. That's right— N-O-R-T-H-A-M-P-T-O-N. Old Don White, Ron Jacobs and I used to have great times when I was at stand-off . . . scissors movements, cross kicks, the lot. The papers all said I was as fast as Lew Cannell, who used to be outside me then, but that's rot. Actually, over a hundred yards Lew could beat me by a good six inches. I said to old Dickie Jeeps last night, I said, "Dickie, old boy, do you realise I have been reserve for more England trials than any other player in the country?" and he just roared. A great chap, old Dickie . . .'

The effect on our opponents was extraordinary. After staring goggle-eyed they went straight into a huddle.

'Listen carefully,' the captain would say, 'you've got to watch that bloke in the odd jersey. It's a Northampton jersey. He used to play stand-off with Lew Cannell outside him.'

All eyes would swivel towards me. A few would express disbelief. 'You mean that chap with the receding hair and a stoop, who's coughing all over the place? He doesn't look as if he played for Northampton.'

'That means nothing. A lot of these great players are a bit weedy. You can see that bloke's

got class all right. Besides, he's been telling me
about how he hob-nobs with Dickie Jeeps.'

'Who does this geezer Jeeps play for?'

'He doesn't play for anyone, you fool. He's
President of the Rugby Union or something
like that. Now listen carefully, here's what we'll
do. If they get the ball from a scrum I want
Ron and Charlie to go straight for this Northampton chap. Then both centres ignore your
own men and come inside to help in case he
jinks through. Meanwhile, George, Bert and
Fred will go for the corner flag. I want Arthur
to come across from the wing and Jack to lie
deep.'

The result was that whenever we heeled and
I scuttled sideways like a frightened crab in my
usual style, the whole opposing side rushed
madly in all directions, waving their arms and
shouting. It was like a medieval siege. I used
to wait a few moments for them to get thoroughly out of position and then pass. As everyone
was marking me, we got through nearly every
time.

Mind you, they tumbled to it eventually,
especially when I had to leave the field to be
sick following a short sprint. But by then we
were twelve points up.

This started a craze for wearing odd jerseys

and in the end we had to stop the practice. It looks rather odd when the Extra B turn up wearing the colours of half a dozen of the most famous clubs in the country. One forward even persuaded his mother to fake up an English jersey.

By the way, never, *never* wear a new jersey. This gives the impression that you have just joined the club or are a tyro at the game. If you can't pinch an old jersey then buy a new one and wash it five times before playing. Or lend it to a man in the First XV to dirty it for you. They like clean jerseys in the First XV.

All jerseys should, if possible, be tattered and faded. If they can be torn and clumsily stitched, so much the better. I have known countless games won because the appearance of a team was so frightening that their opponents were nine points down before they got on to the field

Also, if the stitching is weak and the jersey is grasped in a tackle, it comes away easily, leaving the would-be tackler foolishly holding a piece of cloth while his victim sprints for the line.

Shorts should never be brief. Leave that sort of thing to the Continentals. Shorts (or trousers as I prefer to call them) should be long enough to cover the knees in case of cold weather, and sufficiently baggy for the wearer to thrust in his hands in comfort, to warm them. They should have a large pocket, big enough for a packet of cigarettes and a book of safety matches in case you feel like a smoke at half-time or during a break in play, such as when lining up for a conversion or when a player is injured.

A friend was once seized by the waist of his shorts while at full speed and they split from front to back down the seam. He repaired them himself in a very rough fashion and a few games later the same thing happened. But this time his stitching was so weak that the shorts simply fell apart and he was able to continue his run, falling over the line for a try half-naked. I commend the idea, because coarse players prefer to tackle by the clothes whenever possible.

Socks (if worn) should be of odd colours and one should be worn up and the other down. On no account wear elastic or tape round the tops of the socks, as this stops them from falling down.

Boots will have studs with projecting nails. It is impossible to avoid this. Shopkeepers stock a special Coarse boot in which the nails after one game either shoot downwards through the stud or upwards into the foot. As all the opposition will have similar boots do not worry. It is just as well to have some method of retaliation. Perhaps the best compromise is to have just one projecting nail then no one will be scratched —except deliberately.

Laces should never be full length. A good test is whether or not you have to bend the metal tag in an effort to do them up. The lace should end halfway up the boot. The more frequently it comes undone, the better, as this gives the excuse for a rest.

The general demeanour of a side before the game is most important. Not everyone can be big, but anyone can *look* big. Remember Green's Law, which says that the opposition in any game always look bigger than you, irrespective of their actual size.

Do not shave on the morning of a game. Put pieces of sticking-plaster over imaginary wounds on the face and knees. Spit loudly and frequently. Talk volubly of the thrashing you have inflicted on other teams. If the other side make conversation, reply in ape-like grunts. Let us have none of this 'Glad to see your lot again, old man' chatter. Make them feel like unwanted guests at some cannibal feast. In short, BE SUB-HUMAN.

4

'They are hanging their jackets, and all who mean real work, their hats, waistcoats, neck-handkerchiefs, and braces, on the railings . . .'—Tom Brown's Schooldays.

If all the splendid wheezes mentioned in the previous chapter are carried out a team will be well on the way to success before a single kick is made. However, there is still much that can be done before the match starts.

Most Coarse Rugby grounds are reached after a long walk through depressing surroundings. For some reason they inevitably have an electric pylon beside them. Why this should be I do not know, but there is always a pylon beside the Extra B pitch. I have never been able to think of a way of turning this to advantage. Can any reader suggest a use for electric pylons? There must be one.*

* A reader has since written to say that there *is* a use for electric cables. One of his side kicked the ball up among them whereupon it disappeared in a cloud of blue smoke, thus ending the game and blacking-out half the town.

This walk is a time of acute nervousness for both sides, but especially for the opponents who are already demoralised by previous tactics, and who are not on familiar ground. It is important to keep them depressed.

Walk boldly, talk loudly of exploits at boxing, wrestling, judo, brawling and rugby. Recall past successes, real or imaginary. Adopt a general air of bravado. Remember that Napoleon said the moral is to the physical as three is to one. Let boldness be your friend.

Teams which play on public parks often have to put up their own goalposts. If this is so, try to make the opponents carry the posts to the ground. It is quite easy to do this—just give all the posts to one of the home side, and if he totters round in circles making a great fuss about it the visitors will feel sorry for him and offer to help. With luck this will tire them a little and there is always the chance they will drop a post on someone's toe.

But *never* allow the other side to erect posts and crossbars, because this can be turned to advantage. For instance, if the crossbar is not placed properly in the slot it will fall down if a ball strikes the bar or the posts

Your side, of course, know this and keep well clear of the crossbar. But the opposition see no danger. Let me give an example to show how this can be turned to good use.

Near the end of a close game we were losing by two points. There was a five-yard scrum immediately in front of the posts and our pack pushed the other set of forwards back to their line, but not quite far enough for a pushover try. Heeling was useless because we had only eleven men and we had put most of the backs into the pack for a supreme effort.

Just at the vital moment our scrum-half happened to knock against the post. The crossbar came straight down on the opposing pack, two of them collapsed and we pushed over for the winning try.

In another game we deliberately foiled a penalty kick by shaking the posts unobtrusively, causing the crossbar to fall down just as the ball was about to pass over it. The referee could find no rule to cover the incident so he had the kick taken again and this time it missed. We were rather proud of this wheeze.

It is not always necessary to jog the crossbar down. I was called in to referee a match in which a penalty kick was foiled by pushing a loose post so hard that the top of it moved sufficiently for the ball to pass outside. This move was perpetrated by several great heroes of

Coarse Rugby, including my brother Roger, who were playing for the local Over-Thirties against the Under-Thirties on Boxing Day.

Being over thirty myself I naturally disallowed the kick and some of the youngsters were a little annoyed. But the matter of the kick was a mild business compared with some of the tactics. To start with, one of the veterans was under a year's suspension by the local union for persistent foul play, and we were all liable to be suspended for playing with him, so I shan't go into any more detail.

I played in one park game in which the crossbar fell down when an attempted conversion hit it and knocked five men unconscious. What's more, the referee added insult to injury by allowing the conversion.

This particular way of knocking down the crossbar is of little practical value, except as a way of getting revenge on the opposition. An exceptionally good kicker might aim at the crossbar or a post with the intention of concussing half-a-dozen opponents. Worth remembering for a dirty game in which there are many old scores to pay off, as they could all be settled at once, instead of having to deal with individual players. And they cannot retaliate.

I need hardly emphasise the importance of

never standing underneath the crossbar.

A final word about posts. When a player had an attack of nose-bleeding some blood was accidentally splattered over our posts. It was left for years as a silent warning to opponents. If they asked how it came there we simply said we didn't want to talk about it, life was for the living and there was enough tragedy in the world without dwelling on the past.

Many coarse teams do not bother with such refinements as halfway and corner flags. That is a big mistake as these inanimate objects can be made to work for you. As soon as the toss has been made, and ends chosen, move the corner flags inside the line a few inches. Dig them in very lightly so they fall down at the slightest touch. This can be done by the full-back, touch-judge (if any) or a friendly spectator. The opposition will be doing the same, so have no qualms.

This wheeze can make all the difference between a winger's scoring and being ruled in touch ('Bad luck, old boy, you just touched the post'). If this should happen, by the way, try to ensure that the post is well and truly knocked over so that no one spots it was not in its proper place. And, of course, replace it as before.

It is hardly necessary to say that whenever

tackling an opponent in the corner, one should always try to knock down the corner post, so that the referee thinks the man with the ball touched it. Watch any international match to see how to do this.

As regards the pitch itself, this should be as small as possible—about ten yards each way smaller than the minimum laid down in the Laws. I say without any hesitation that big pitches are the curse of Coarse Rugby. It is quite unfair to expect people in bad physical condition to chase each other all afternoon in a huge arena the size of a public park.

The geographical location of the ground can also be used to advantage, but some preparation before the game is necessary.

Most coarse grounds are near a river, stream, canal or open sewer (is it because the ground is so waterlogged as to be unfit for anything else?). If the ball is kicked into one of these when a team are winning, a breathing-space is gained. And the lost time can never be made up because coarse games begin so late that darkness inevitably applies the closure with several minutes to go. The danger is that the other side will adapt the same tactics.

Always, therefore, have a forked stick or a net on a long handle by the side of the water, so that the ball can be recovered as soon as possible, if it suits you. But as soon as you get into the lead, and the game is drawing to a close, *hide the forked stick*. Perhaps a player can do it under the pretext of retrieving the ball. Or a spectator might. But it must be done secretly.

Try to avoid what happened when a player did this and a small boy came up and said loudly, 'Hey mister, do you want that forked stick to get the ball?'

The player who had carefully concealed it in the bushes, hissed, 'Go away, sonny,' viciously, but without effect.

'It's right by you in the bushes,' bellowed the child in a voice loud enough to be heard all over the field. He went on: 'Hey mister, why are you hissing and winking at me like that? Why are you winking, mister? Why are you winking, mister? Why——.' He got no further because he suddenly vanished into the bushes with a howl, but the damage was done. The ball was immediately retrieved and the team lost by a try scored in the last minute. Which shows how important this can be.

I once played for a side who used an old boat to retrieve balls from the canal. The bravest act I have ever seen in rugby was performed by our captain who deliberately overturned the boat in midstream in an effort to delay the resumption of play.

It is presumed, of course, that there is no spare ball, or that you arrange to lose or hide it early on.

A railway line near the ground gives wonderful opportunities for delay. Just boot the ball over it and then warn everyone not to cross because the 3.40 is due any minute and last week it mowed down the full-back when he was fetching the ball.

When the 3.40 doesn't appear, make a great pantomime of looking both ways up and down the line and of putting your ear to the rail. Then tip-toe cautiously across.

Of course, if *you're* losing and the ball goes across the line, life and limb don't matter. I have seen men fly in front of express trains and dive into rivers to get the ball when they're behind.

One of my clubs used to have a field next door with a bull in it, which saved us any subterfuge. If we kicked the ball into the field it couldn't be retrieved and that was an end of it. Later the farmer put cows in the field, but we still kept up the pretence until one of the other side remarked that the bulls seemed physically deformed, and then the game was up in both senses.

Perhaps an imaginary bull is better than a real one. A big notice with BEWARE OF THE BULL and a skull and crossbones is enough. Then if it suits you to retrieve the ball, say the bull was removed years ago.

There is a further way of cutting short a game in which you are winning, but it only applies to public parks. The park-keeper may be persuaded to come along ten minutes from the end and tell the referee the game has to stop, because he's closing the park. I have been on the wrong end of this wheeze, and I'm sure they had bribed the park-keeper, because it was still broad daylight. Of course, it is essential that the park-keeper comes only when the side are winning. It would be a little awkward if he insisted on stopping the game when you were three points down and pressing hard.

Another important piece of preparation before the match concerns the ball. If your strength lies in your pack, deflate the ball so that it is well suited to forward rushes and less suited to passing. On the other hand, if the enemy have a strong pack, inflate the ball hard so that its liveliness will make it difficult to control in a foot rush. Ideally, there should be a new ball available if your strength lies behind the scrum, but coarse sides are never allowed to play with a new ball. It is important not to let the opposition see the match ball before play or they may attempt to blow it up or de-flate it.

Every possible preparation has been made and the team take the field. Yet still more can be done before play starts.

First, DO NOT INDULGE IN A WARM-UP.

Countless games have been lost because of this foolish habit. It is impossible to exaggerate the boost the other side receive from seeing their opponents throwing the ball to each other and dropping it, taking kicks at goal and missing by miles, or doing all-out sprints at walking pace.

Instead of warming up, concentrate on de-pressing the opponents. The best kicker in the side should take a series of shots at goal from in front of the posts and about 20 yards out. As even a Coarse Rugby player should get about 25 per cent of these over, the other side will be scared of giving away penalty kicks.

The forwards should stand still, glaring to-wards the other side with curling lips and snarling faces. If the enemy kick the ball in their direction, let them come and fetch it themselves. Spit occasionally.

The backs should pretend to be planning fantastic tactical moves. It is best if they gather round the fly-half, who can use his hands expressively, like an R.A.F. pilot shooting a line. Wave the hands to indicate men criss-crossing each other, jinking sideways and bursting through. The other backs should nod sagely and jig up and down eagerly as if they can't wait to put these moves into operation. As a final gesture the fly-half does an imitation of a savage hand-off with the heel of the hand, and everyone nods and looks fierce.

Meanwhile, the referee, if any, will be asking the captains how long they want to play. In this connection I must protest against the tendency which has grown in recent years for games to last forty minutes each way. This is a typical rugger move, based on the fallacy that the game is played by fit supermen with energy to burn, leading lives of monk-like celibacy and temperance.

But to expect the sort of person who plays Coarse Rugby, perhaps an undersized youth or a flabby clerk, to play forty minutes each way is not only cruel, it is dangerous. An ideal period would be twenty minutes each way with an interval of fifteen minutes in which drinks are served, but as tradition seems against this, it is the duty of every captain to bargain with the referee for the shortest possible playing period.

Occasionally a referee who has strayed from a higher sphere will hopefully suggest to the captains, 'Forty minutes each way?'

This should be met with a howl of derisive laughter and a counter-suggestion is made of twenty-five minutes each way with ten minutes' break at half-time. This is purely a bargaining suggestion, like the initial price asked when selling a car. Although it is meant seriously, the referee won't take it that way. It is up to him to make his bid now, which is invariably thirty-five minutes.

The home captain points out that it gets dark around here very early and that if they go on too long there won't be any tea left, because the other teams will have scoffed it. This leaves the gate open for possible negotiations at half-time (which is nowhere near the middle of the game). The referee makes a mental note to play only thirty minutes, but for the sake of appearances sticks at thirty-five.

A captain who wins the toss should always play with the wind or slope in his favour for the first half, as the first half is invariably much longer than the second. This is because of the

Occasionally a referee who has strayed from a higher sphere will hopefully suggest to the captains, 'Forty minutes each way?'

late kick-off, but is also caused by the unfitness of the average coarse referee, who's had enough long before the end and is glad to end it all. On

an average I should say that the first half of
the average coarse game lasts thirty-one minutes and the second half twenty-six minutes, so
you gain five minutes advantage.

Whether wind or slope is a bigger help is a
problem. Personally, I always favour the slope,
because touch-kicking is at such a low ebb that
a team never make proper use of the wind,
whereas the slope is kind to ageing limbs and
gives an illusion of vigour to the unfit (i.e.
everyone in the team).

One captain always chose ends so that in the
second half his team defended the end nearer
the dressing-room. This was one of those
ghastly grounds shared by twelve teams and it
was the only way to ensure that the bath water
was hot. Probably that's as good a reason as
any for making a choice, and a good deal better
than some.

If the toss is lost, it is important to pretend
that the opponents' choice suits your team.
The captain should call out clearly, 'O.K.,
chaps, they've played right into our hands.
That's just what we wanted. We've a great
chance this half,' and give the thumbs-up sign.
With luck, the enemy will feel their skipper has
bungled the whole affair, and a sense of defeat
will spread.

In fact anything that can be done either before or during a game to cause a split between their captain and his team should be done. A quiet word at half-time or during a break for an injury can do untold damage. Just a remark like, 'Right-ho, chaps, they've made a fatal mistake switching those centres, the plan has worked perfectly,' can send doubt and distrust sweeping through the enemy.

One should also directly attack the captain in his capacity as a player and suggest that he is the weak link in the other team (he probably is, anyway). For instance, if their skipper is fly-half, shout, 'Don't bother about the fly-half, chaps, go for the centres. The fly-half won't score, don't worry about him.' It is a strong man who can stand up to that sort of stuff. His game will probably go to pieces.

It is interesting to note, by the way, that when a skipper's game goes to pieces he takes it out on the rest of his side, so that morale generally is shattered.

This wheeze can be used to attack any individual player on the other side. Select one who is obviously slightly off form and hammer him mercilessly. Roar with laughter when he drops a pass, groan when he muffs a kick, loudly tell the team not to bother to mark him, ask him if he feels ill, or would he like to leave the field? In short, SHATTER HIM.

It is surprising how strong the herd instinct is in rugby. If you persevere long enough at one man, his own side will eventually turn on him and start blaming him for all their troubles. They will be heard bickering as they line-up for a conversion. And when a team starts doing that, all is lost.

5

'Here come Speedicut, and Flashman the School-house bully, with shouts and great action . . .'—Tom Brown's School-days.

With luck, and if the various wheezes have been properly performed, the game will be won without much of this disagreeable running about which spoils so much rugby these days. However, quite often the winning wheezes have to be put into action on the field of play.

Tactics in Coarse Rugby are different from those used in rugger. They are dictated by the lack of energy, ability and often enthusiasm of the players. But by far the most important factor is that neither side ever has fifteen men. A team's status can be judged by the number of its players, in the same way as some African tribes judge a man's status by the number of his wives.

In a game with thirteen men on each side, it's a safe bet that they are the third teams of two good clubs, or the second teams of two not-so-good clubs. If you see a match with nine men on each side then you may be sure they are the fifth or sixth teams. Obviously a game with fifteen a side is between two first XVs.

Since so much rugby is played below strength I wonder that the Rugby Union do not invent a special game to be played by twelve men or fewer, but adaptable to any number. Actually, such a game is being formed by tradition and necessity. Perhaps the Laws could be amended to help it.

For instance Law 12, which says a match shall be played by not more than fifteen players in each team, could be amended to read: 'ANY NUMBER CAN PLAY.'

Then, if four coarse teams all turn up short they could combine into one jolly little game of twenty-one a-side. Think of the ease and peace it would bring to elderly legs to have more men on each side. Instead of scratching round all week to try to fill up the Extra C, etc., a club could combine all its coarse teams into one enormous side of about forty players, who would play forty from another club.

If one side was a few short it would not matter among so many. Perhaps to add interest two balls could be used. *I am not joking.* Something must be done to make rugby more suitable for older players.

Then there is the matter of scoring (Law 7). This emphasis on scoring tries and goals is all wrong. It leads to a lot of running about. I suggest that the try should be cut down to one point, with one further point for a conversion, and the penalty goal increased to five points. The drop goal would be abolished. A new way of scoring would be introduced. Ten points would be awarded for punting the ball over the crossbar. This would be known as a 'punt-goal'. After every punt-goal both sides would change round and have two minutes' rest.

All this deals with theory, but there are still alterations to the Laws which need to be made to suit the present game. For instance, Law 5, relating to players' dress, needs an addition which forbids a player to carry non-safety matches in his shorts, owing to the danger of fire in the scrum. If you have ever seen a fire in a scrum, you will not laugh at this. It is no joke when a player's shorts burst into flames and turn the pack into a holocaust.

Of course, someone must have matches, or nobody could smoke during a game. But they must either be safety matches, or they should be left just behind the posts, where they come in handy for a quick drag during a conversion.

Perhaps two balls could be used . .

Then there are Laws 34 and 35, which stip-
ulate offences for which a player *must* be sent
off and what the referee should do after the
game. Well, there's no point in sending a man
off in Coarse Rugby, because he doesn't merely
go into the dressing-room as in rugger, he

stands on the touch-line shouting at all and sundry and generally making a nuisance of himself. A referee who sent off one of our men had to call him back, he made such a fuss. 'Will you behave if I let you come back?' he asked him, and the man of course said yes, so back he came.

Another player was sent off in the first ten minutes and merely walked over to an adjacent pitch and got a game there. The referee could see him playing, and couldn't do anything about it. In fact he was nearly sent off in the other game.

One could quote other instances where the Laws need amending, or have fallen into disrepute. Perhaps one day Coarse Rugby will have its own legislator, some third team Hampden who will perform this service.

Coarse Rugby teams are so used to playing three or four short that they automatically adjust the composition of the team to suit the number of players. A first-class rugger side, if it loses a back, or even two, slavishly pulls a player out of the pack. A skilful coarse side, however, is constantly switching its depleted resources between forwards and backs so that at one time it may have a full pack and only three backs, while on other occasions there will be only three forwards and everyone else will be in the backs.

After all, if you're going to lose possession anyway, there's not much point in wasting men in the pack, is there?

It is very rare for either side to be complete, so a team which is three short may be at a disadvantage of only one player, or even at an advantage numerically. If we were four short, giving us eleven to our opponents' twelve, we put both wingers and the full-back into the pack in defence. That gave seven forwards to our opponents' five (unless they knew the wheeze), so we ensured possession and the scrum-half would kick us out of trouble.

In mid-field, however, we played only four forwards, because when we lost the scrum it was ten to one the other side would knock on or pass forward or make a hash of it in some way. In attack we absolutely denuded the scrum, reducing it to three men, the minimum allowed. (I hope they change that Law. I look forward to the day of the one-man pack.) Of course we lost the ball, but it didn't do the opposition any good. We outnumbered them nearly two-to-one in the outsides and it was easy to rattle them into a mistake and sweep through. They looked dreadfully puzzled.

Their full-back even counted our men as if he could not believe it. He was still counting when we scored.

A lot of the success of moves like this depends entirely on mistakes by the opposition backs. This, however, is not a matter of chance, but of certainty. They *will* make a mistake. That is why they are in the Extra B.

In rugger, if one set of backs secures the ball, and no one interferes, they will usually score. But in Coarse Rugby, give some backs the ball, remove their opponents, tell them to run fifty yards, making two passes, and then score, AND THEY WILL FAIL SEVEN TIMES OUT OF TEN.

Probably the fly-half will knock on the pass from the scrum, or else it will go nowhere near him. Certainly one of the centres will fumble, and if he doesn't, he will pass forward.

It is astonishing the ingenious lengths that players go to *not* to score. I have seen men kick for touch when they were six feet from an undefended line. I've not only seen it, I've done it myself. A kind of madness creeps over you, a conviction you'll never make it, or else one imagines opponents that aren't there. I have also seen players pass three feet and still manage to hit a colleague on the head or throw the ball at his feet. Even if a coarse back crosses the line, that is no guarantee that he will score. He will probably drop the ball, or run over the dead ball line. Like a friend who touched down on a soccer pitch at the end of the ground. Admittedly there was a slight mist at the time.

I have touched down behind the 25 line by mistake. I thundered along, flung myself over the 25 line triumphantly and got up with a swagger. Next moment half a dozen forwards knocked me flat on my back. I didn't realise what had happened and leaped up crying, 'Swines, you'll suffer for this, filthy beasts,' etc., etc. It took hours to pacify me and explain what had happened.

One thing is certain. *The ball will never reach the wing.*

Wings in Coarse Rugby are not attacking players at all. In fact they are rarely even players. The wing is a sort of repository for cripples, injured players, old men, timid young-sters, and the spectator who volunteered to play. His only duties are to throw in the ball and fill any gaps which may arise.

Note that all the mistakes I have outlined occur without any opposition. Most moves will break down without anyone doing anything at all. All opponents could leave the field and they would still break down. But the mere

presence of a defender or two enormously in-
creases the possibility of successful defence.

All one needs to break up most coarse threequarter moves is to stand opposite your man
and wave the arms. Without you he would
probably knock-on. With you there he certainly
will. Coarse Rugby players have some brain
defect which makes it impossible for them not
to look at their opponents. They stare mesmer-
ised and let the ball slip from their nerveless
fingers, as the novels say.

If you stand perfectly still, just waving the
arms to attract attention, an opponent will
eventually run into you. Players will swerve ten
yards out of their way to run straight into a defender. They are like rabbits facing a stoat.

It reminds me of a schoolboy story before the
war in which a soccer team played a man who
was a hypnotist and he used to mesmerise the
goalkeeper before he shot. They had drawings
of him about to shoot, with zig-zag lightning
flashes coming out of the ends of his fingers and
the goalkeeper looking glassy-eyed. It made a
great impression on me and I spent hours trying
to make zig-zag flashes come out of my fingers.
But I didn't realise at the time how near the
truth it was.

For this reason, possession of the ball is not

Stand opposite your man and wave the arms.

very important in Coarse Rugby, except when very near your own line and there is the danger an opponent may accidentally cross it.

In fact, one usually does *better* when the opposition have the ball. As long as they have it there's a good chance of a knock-on or forward pass, or that the ball will go loose and you can seize it and charge through. There's nothing bucks up a side so much as seeing their opponents passing the ball back and back, losing ground all the time and finishing up with a knock-on in front of the posts.

However, sometimes possession is essential, especially if a team are really heavily outnumbered, as in one game in which we had ten men to the enemy's thirteen. But we still won, thanks to some tactical play.

The danger was not in the scrum. The other backs were so bad that time and time again I stopped them single-handed from full-back simply by shouting and waving my arms and jumping up and down. They always knocked on when they were still in the distance.

No, the danger lay in the line-outs, because by accident or design they adopted the French style and struggled right back across the field and our depleted side couldn't possibly mark their men under those circumstances. At all costs line-outs had to be avoided

When forced near the line we put every able-bodied man in the pack to ensure possession and left the other two as halves. Their instructions were to make as much ground as possible without kicking and then deliberately commit an offence which would result in a scrum. We could guarantee winning the scrums, but not the line-outs.

It was difficult to pick a suitable offence, because we could no more afford penalties than line-outs. It was useless giving an opponent an uppercut under the chin. At the same time we had to pick an offence which did not involve the advantage rule, so it was no good simply hurling the ball forward and looking hopefully at the referee.

To commit the right type of offence required great talent and considerable acting ability.

The favourite offences were:

Accidental Offside: This was a beauty, because there was little danger of advantage being played. It would have done old Stanislavsky's heart good to see the way our two halves managed to run into each other, cursing and swearing and telling each other to get out of the way. (See Fig. 1.)

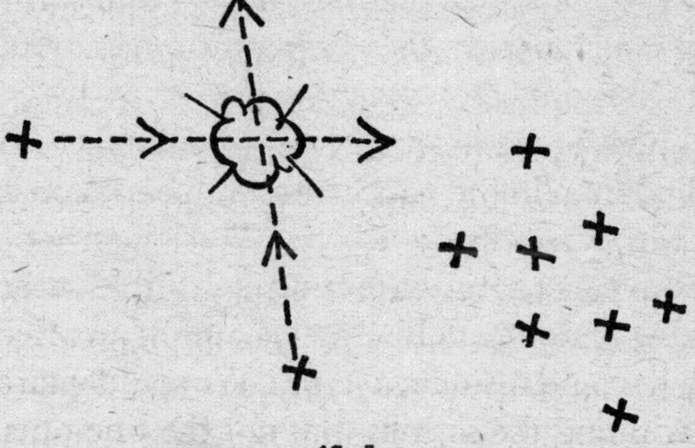

Fig. 1.

Ball Striking Referee: Another great idea a simply splendid wheeze, a positive piece of inspiration invented by that great Coarse Rugby genius Slasher Williams, with whom I have played many a great game. I well recall the first time it was used.

Slasher (so called because of his habit of letting his nails grow long in the rugby season) had become completely isolated from the rest of the side as he knelt down on all fours to recover his breath, when the opposition broke away near the half-way line. They kicked ahead and the ball came near Slasher. By the time he had recovered himself, three opponents were bearing down on him and not one of his own side was within fifty yards (we had all given it up as a bad job). There was not even time to kick.

Quick as a flash he hurled the ball twenty yards at the referee and struck him straight between the shoulder blades (as usual, he had his back to play). The referee blew up immediately and the situation was saved.

Mind you, it is not always easy to do this. Sometimes a player runs so far ahead of the referee he has to stooge around in midfield until the ref catches up. Ideally, one should throw the ball as hard as possible. There is always the chance of hitting him in the stomach and he will collapse, winded. Then you might seize the chance to have the game abandoned.

Often, by the way, it is possible to make a lot of ground by running behind the referee. This was discovered accidentally when Taffy Owen, one of those wizened little Welshmen in every side, found the referee jogging along in front of him. Being short-sighted he was looking all over the field for the ball.

Taff said nothing but just continued to trot quietly behind him. He made sixty yards before the opposition twigged what was happening and discovered where the ball was. When they threatened him he caught up with the referee and bounced the ball on his head.

He was a dear old soul. 'Good gracious me, I wondered where it was,' he said, and blew for a scrum.

That is rugby to me. I'd like to see some of those swank international players show the same sort of ingenuity. It was a great loss to the game when Taff was sued over a second-hand car and had to leave town hurriedly. I often wonder what he's doing now.

Sometimes the referee looks surprised or even frightened when he sees a player chasing him all over the field, with grim determination on his face. He wonders if he has offended anyone and may try to escape. But don't weaken. Keep at it. He may even blow his whistle out of sheer fright. I have known it happen.

Dropping the Ball: This is not so good a wheeze as the first two, because there is always the danger that the referee will allow the advantage rule. It is best to drop the ball, try to pick it up, do a fumbling scoop which will stop the other side getting it, and finally sit on it. I don't see how even a coarse referee could ignore that one, but it is hardly worth a penalty. Of course, make it look quite accidental when you sit on the ball.

Feigning Injury: Definitely to be used in emergencies only. The technique is quite simple. When all else fails and you are surrounded on your own line by five opponents with none of your own men to hand, just collapse, shrieking. 'Oh, my ankle, quick, someone, do something quick, the pain's killing me, the zongular tendon's gone again, aaaaaaahhhhhh. . . .'

The referee is supposed to blow up for injury only when there is a stoppage, but if your shrieks are sufficiently convincing the other side may put the ball into touch out of sheer pity for the gibbering wreck on the ground, and then, of course, it is your turn to throw it in.

But you *must* sustain the act. We adopted this

wheeze once and as soon as the ball went into touch the man who was feigning injury jumped up all smiles and said, 'Ah, it's better now. Let's get on with the game.'

The referee, who had a nasty, suspicious mind, did not believe that he had been hurt at all and an unpleasant scene ensued, as a result of which soon afterwards the referee allowed a try by the other side from a pass which even they admitted was forward.

On the other hand, if a player is too convincing that can lead to equal complications. One man shrieked so convincingly that the referee insisted he left the field, which, as we only had eleven players, was a positive disaster.

The player kept bounding around saying, 'Look, ref, I'm all right, it's suddenly come better, I tell you, it doesn't hurt now, honest, I can play on, just look,' and jumping all over the field like a kangaroo, but the ref insisted he left the field.

He was one of those referees who fancy themselves as doctors and he diagnosed a displaced ankle bone.

'I appreciate you don't want to let the side down,' he told him, 'but I can't allow you to risk that ankle. You might injure yourself for life.' He even insisted that the St. John Ambulance men were called to carry him off on a stretcher.

We lost 35-nil thanks to that, and the player who was carried off was taken all the way to hospital and had to wait three hours while they X-rayed him. It was almost closing time when he got back.

Incidentally, watch these St. John Ambulance people. They mean well, but they can do grave damage. When the local St. John post needed five casualties to make 1,000 for the season, or some record or other, they swooped down like ghouls and decimated us. You had only to fall over and a chap in a black and white cap would come rushing over, pour water down your neck, and literally drag you off

As soon as they had booked you in they lost interest, as you counted in their tally, and then they let you go.

There is, I regret to say, a serious side to this business of feigning injury. Taffy Owen, who was a great hand at pretending to be hurt, used to do it so well that when he was really injured no one would believe him.

He lay down groaning in agony and we merely became impatient and said, 'All right, Taff, it was very good, but don't overdo it.'

We were so tired of his groaning that we

dragged him to his feet and he promptly fell down again. Eventually he had to crawl off the field by himself, like a wounded fox, with jeers ringing in his ears. We still thought he was putting on an act so he could have a rest.

He lay on the touch-line for the rest of the game and it wasn't until we noticed he was unconscious that we suspected his injury might be genuine.

Then we rushed him to hospital where they found he had broken his leg. He was rather cool to us for some time after that.

6

Most of the wheezes described so far are not concerned with obtaining possession of the ball. But there are times when a team will win the ball despite their efforts and it is important to have tactics ready to meet the occasion.

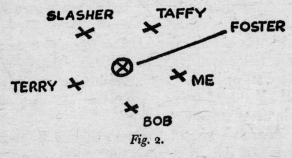

Fig. 2.

The finest threequarter wheeze I know is The Phalanx, or Foster's Phalanx as it is some times known, having been invented by that

Grand Old Man of Coarse Rugby, Tubby Foster. Tubby needed to invent something like this, because although he was a centre three-quarter, his top speed was only three miles an hour.

The original Phalanx was simplicity itself. As soon as Tubby got the ball nine men surrounded him (see Fig. 2) and the whole lot ran towards the line. This formation was almost impenetrable, and if any opponent did force his way inside, he was hidden from the referee and could be dealt with summarily.

This worked fine with the usual referee until he went on a course and learned the Laws. Then he decided that the Phalanx offended Law 20 (f), which prohibits players from wilfully standing in front of their own men to obstruct opponents.

I may say in passing that this shows how over-refinement is dangerous to the game. We were all perfectly happy until the referee went on an absurd series of lectures. Some people can never leave well alone.

After this, we had to adopt a slightly different style. In this, the same nine men formed a shield round Tubby, but they did it much more subtly, zig-zagging and criss-crossing about like nobody's business. They all looked as if they were moving into carefully planned positions, but in fact it was simply the good old game of making it difficult for the opponent to get at Tubby. Fig. 3 shows that I mean.

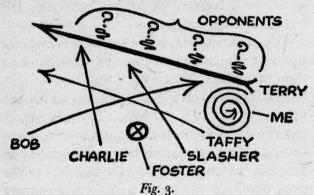

Fig. 3.

If anyone says this is either unfair or impracticable I beg him to look at a photograph of any line-out in the Varsity game, and to tell me why the forwards in possession have all linked arms? Is it to pick buttercups or to protect the scrum-half by obstructing the other forwards? Your guess is as good as mine.

As far as I know there is no certain way of countering either Foster's Phalanx or the Zig-Zag Phalanx, short of a hand grenade, unless you can arrange a counter-phalanx and charge the enemy. The result would be most instructive, but I have yet to see it done.

Taff Owen, before he broke his leg, flung himself flat in front of a phalanx so that they all fell over him. It was rather like those old Keystone Cop films in which someone ties a rope across the pavement and thirty policemen fall over. Very impressive.

The man with the ball also fell over, whereupon we all jumped on him and made sure he didn't try that one again

This was one of the occasions on which the other side were also skilled in Coarse Rugby. I am afraid that confusion is bound to arise when two such teams face each other. As soon as one side sees the other pulling four men out of the pack it will do the same, and then the others try to sneak the men back, so that soon the pitch is a seething mass of players running to and fro while the scrum-half waits to put the ball in.

There is not much one can do about this except to make sure the ball is not put in until you are ready. If the other side have the loose head it is always possible to delay their scrum-half by knocking the ball from his hands and treading on his fingers when he goes to pick it up. Simple, but effective.

One of the jolliest wheezes I know was invented by a tiny scrum-half who used to wear a jersey so long that it came down to his calves.

They all laughed at him until he stuffed the
ball under his jersey after a five-yard scrum and

*. . . knocking the ball from his hands and treading on his
fingers when he goes to pick it up.*

strolled over the line while everyone was running round looking for the ball.

This was his stock trick. He used to do it once every game. They always fell for it, except the sides with a touch-judge intelligent enough to shout out a warning.

He had another trick in defence. If one of the enemy pursued him closely in touch-in-goal, he used to run as hard as he could at one of the posts and then dodge aside at the last moment. The other player usually ran straight into the post. One of them even broke it. We had a lot of laughs over that. The other side didn't see the joke, especially the man who hit the post. I always felt that this scrum-half was worthy of a place in a higher grade of rugby but he refused all promotion. It was discovered later he was under a period of suspension for insulting a referee and had joined us under an assumed name.

While talking of personalities I must refer again to one of Slasher Williams' exploits with feelings amounting almost to reverence and awe. It was an occasion when we had only ten men to our opponents' twelve. Then Slasher wrenched his knee and left the field, unable to stand except on one leg. Within a few minutes the opposition were sweeping down the field for a certain try, when Slasher crawled on to the field from the touch-line and tripped up the winger.

Of course there was an awful row about it. The referee didn't see what happened, and Slasher denied it all. However, it gave him an idea and after that he returned to the field. He couldn't stand properly, so he just crawled all over the pitch, tripping people up whenever he got near. He patrolled a beat along the 25 line on his hands and knees. It was astonishingly effective, because you never think of looking down when running and just as some three-quarter fancied he was through he would find himself flat on his face with old Slasher's hand clutching his ankle.

The referee tried to object but Slasher asked him what Law he was breaking, and he couldn't think of one. The other side were furious and one of them surreptitiously kicked Slasher but Slasher still kept on crawling.

We won handsomely, thanks to Slasher.

So far I have dealt mainly with physical tactics and wheezes but never forget that the human voice, used effectively, can be as good as a tackle.

For instance, if your side scores a doubtful try, launch into loud cries of 'Well done, Vipers, well done. Well scored, Charlie, well touched down, you definitely beat him to it, I saw it clearly. . . .'

It is a strong-minded referee who can withstand that sort of thing, and strong-minded refs are not as a rule in Coarse Rugby.

But whenever a try is scored against your side, cast doubt on it. I must emphasise that this applies to any score whatsoever, not merely tries, but drop and penalty goals as well.

The mock sympathetic and sporting approach is probably best, rather than blatantly appealing to the referee. Something like, 'Bad luck, old man, you deserved a try after a run like that,' or in the case of a kick, 'Bad luck, Old Rottinghamians, just outside the post.'

Follow up promptly by lining up for a 25 drop-out, whatever the referee does. If he insists it is a try show a great deal of hurt surprise and disappointment. He may feel upset at having made the decison against you, and you will get the benefit of the next one.

The same applies if your side score a doubtful try. Everyone should double back to the centre of the field without waiting. Let the place kicker instantly select his mark. If the referee still disallows the try, return with the air of martyrs, but at this stage don't try to intimidate the referee.

Intimidation and open complaints are clumsy forms of persuasion, to be shunned by the true coarse player. A continual brainwashing is much more successful.

Half-time gives great opportunities. The referee feels rather lonely then and it is a good chance to play on his nerves. The smoothest talker can sidle up and say something like: 'By the way, sir, I thought it was a jolly clever decision when you disallowed our try. A lot of our chaps are saying it *was* a try and we're going to lose our unbeaten record because of you, but I think you could have been right. I like the way you stuck to your guns, even though that chap on the touch-line disagreed. These old county players don't know anything about it anyway. . . .'

If all else fails, intimidation may be tried, but only as a last resort. A loud remark like, 'Never mind, Vipers, we'll be reporting it to the Referees' Society,' may make some impression.

Finally, there is sheer bluff. When we lost a game by a dubious conversion, we simply pretended that the kick had failed. We convinced the other side that they had mistaken the referee's decision. The referee himself was a tougher nut, but we told him the result of the match was none of his business, and we were going to put it in our records as a win and that was that.

It is always useful to have a first-aid expert in the team. Not to heal the injured, but to order the removal of hurt opponents, whether they need it or not.

I knew a chap with a little pseudo-medical jargon who was splendid at this. Whenever an opponent was injured he diagnosed some dreadful hurt and ordered his instant removal with an air of authority. This is a superb way of getting rid of dangerous men for a few minutes.

This will work only if the referee knows little about first-aid. In reality, very few of them do. They make a great show of knowledge, telling everyone to stand back and give him air, but it's all bluff. They have only two cures—to bend the unfortunate player up and down (this is wonderful if you have broken a rib) or to rub the back of his neck (I never know why this is done, but it feels nice). So anyone with a little knowledge and confident air can bluff the referee as well as the player.

Generally speaking, one should never be afraid of trying a wheeze through fear of the referee. It is fairly safe to presume he doesn't really know much about it.

I remember a match played on some dismal swamp in East London in which we were quite undeservedly winning by two points when the opposition stand-off broke away and certainly would have scored if our scrum-half, a real hero, had not tripped him up well out on the 25.

The referee ran up wagging his finger. But he didn't award a penalty try. He gave our enraged opponents a penalty kick which they never had a hope of putting over. So we won, all because our scrum-half had the courage and ingenuity to take a risk. A real example to all youngsters who aspire to play Coarse Rugby.

Finally, a word of advice about training.

Don't.

It is difficult to exaggerate the harm which training causes to Coarse Rugby players. In their state of health such violent exercise can be dangerous. The over-exertion can weaken the heart and strain the vital organs.

Have you ever considered that more injuries are caused by training than by playing? The England team no sooner get together before an international than some reckless fool strains his ankle during practice, and loses his place in the team, perhaps for good.

I have, of course, always religiously followed my own advice, although I must admit to trying this training lark one season. It was when they put me in the Second XV. I can't think how that happened. I must have gone beserk or something. However, having had this honour thrust upon me I decided I ought to train, so I turned up one Thursday at the local grammar school, where we used to borrow the gymnasium.

It was awful—much more strenuous than a game. The school gym master was in charge and he made the Count de Sade look like a professional do-gooder. He just tortured us—there's no other word for it.

It was heart-rending to see poor, fat fellows, who should have been at home with their children in front of the television, stumbling round the gym with their stomachs and cheeks wobbling and sweat streaming off them. Then by contrast there were pathetic, thin little chaps being crushed against the parallel bars during some sadistic game called all-in in which everyone tries to kill everyone else.

Personally I am convinced that some of the exercises could lead to a hernia in later life.

It was so awful that, taking advantage of a torture in which we all had to run round the gym, I slipped into a little storeroom to hide, and found half the Extra B there having a smoke.

And that training session proved my point. The First XV skipper, who was rushing round in a very enthusiastic fashion, twisted his knee during some exercise which involved tying himself into a knot and couldn't play for three weeks. All through training.

Did I feel better for the exercise? Of course not. When I went on to the field on Saturday I still felt as if I had been run over by a tram and cleaned up at the hospital with barbed wire. I limped all afternoon and played my worst game for years. I doubt if I shall ever fully recover.

If some sort of mid-week preparation is thought advisable, why not have something useful, such as a series of lectures on Law? This is quite a complicated subject. A solicitor in our side was tremendously useful when things got out of hand. I especially recall one bit of bother in Sussex when some of the lads were trying to remove a sign from a public lavatory and two policemen, not unnaturally, asked them what they were doing.

They were both about to give the game away, when the solicitor said firmly: 'Say nothing. You are not obliged to say anything.'

You see, people don't realise that most offenders are convicted out of their own mouths. The very sight of a copper brings out all the suppressed father-desire in the poor defaulter who stumbles through one of those statements which sound so absurd when they are read tonelessly in court ('That is right, officer, I was in drink, I done it. It is these headaches. I couldn't stand it no more. They can't hang me if he isn't dead, can they?).

Confronted by a wall of silence the two policemen were baffled.

'Ah,' said one eventually, approaching the solicitor. 'May I ask if you are a solicitor by any chance?'

'I decline to make any statement,' replied the solicitor.

'That means you *must* be a solicitor.'

'I do not wish to say anything.'

'Oh ho.'

The policeman could think of nothing to say but 'Oh ho,' which he repeated several times. He and his colleague spent a good deal of time lurking around the coach but didn't trouble us again, much to the relief of two policemen in our team. I think they feared they had stumbled on the annual booze-up of the Judges Friendly Society.

Now how about asking a solicitor to lecture the team on the Law, particularly as it relates to public-houses and drinking offences? Surely it is better and healthier to spend a Thursday evening with a lecture on the rights of the citizen rather than to rush round some stuffy gymnasium?

While on the subject, a representative from the local brewery will be happy to lecture you on the fascinating topic of how beer is brewed, together with legal aspect of drinking. A knowledge of closing times in different parts of the country, together with a list of clubs where drink can be obtained after hours, is a must for the coarse player.

A programme of choral training is another suitable subject for study. Stick to a repertoire of two or three fairly uncommon songs and rehearse them until you are perfect. Then you will have nothing to fear when the call goes up, 'We call on the Vipers to sing us a song,' and all the dire penalties mentioned in that verse.

Some training can be undertaken with direct reference to the game itself. For instance, you might like to practise scrummaging with only four forwards; how to trip a man up and pretend it was an accident; a one-man line-out; and five different ways of tackling someone round the neck.

Personally, I feel the finest training for a coarse player is to join the local amateur dramatic society. Here one can pick up invaluable tips in such useful arts as feigning injury or righteous indignation, and congratulating an opponent while making it perfectly clear you hate his guts.

And now here is a little quiz by which the reader may test his knowledge of Coarse Rugby tactics.

Score two points for each question correctly answered, and one for a half-correct answer. Score ratings: Over twelve—A positive ornament to the game; should go far. You will probably finish up as a Rugby League scout or secretary of a Welsh valley club. Seven to eleven—Not bad, but try to realise you're not in the first team any more. Three to six—You creeping swine, you want to get into a higher side. Serve you right if you do. Under three— I don't want to know you.

1. Your opponents are making a conversion bang in front of the posts. Do you (a)

Make faces at the kicker; (b) All shout, 'Bad luck, just missed,' as the ball goes over; (c) Charge the kicker.

2. An opponent is winded. Do you (a) Diagnose appendicitis and carry him off; (b) Help him to his feet; (c) Bend him up and down so violently that he becomes really ill.

3. You are winning ten minutes from no-side. Do you (a) Puncture the ball; (b) Kick the ball into the nearest field; (c) Signal to the park-keeper to stop the game.

4. The other side score a dubious try. Do you (a) Accept the referee's decision; (b) Strike the referee; (c) Say loudly in the referee's hearing, 'I presume he hasn't read Law 14.'

5. You are winning by two points, with five minutes to go. There is a scrum on the halfway line. Do you (a) Try to heel; (b) Try to take; (c) Let them gain possession of the ball.

6. You are running with the ball in mid-field and you are half-tackled. Do you (a) Shake off the tackler and press on; (b) Give up; (c) Shout, 'You rotten lout, you've punched me in the stomach again,' and collapse, groaning.

7. You are running with the ball and after

twenty yards are too fagged to continue. There is no opponent near. Do you (a) Pretend to stumble and drop the ball; (b) Keep going; (c) Feign illness.

Answers: 1 (b). In the other two cases the kick may be allowed again. One presumes there were no touch-judges. 2 (a). This way you ensure that he leaves the field with no stigma attached to your side. 3 (a). There may be no field, or no park-keeper, but you can always keep a tiny penknife in your shorts for this purpose and wait till the ball is kicked well into touch. 4 (c). The ref won't alter his decision, but this may unsettle him so he gives the next one in your favour. 5 (c). If the scrum is on the halfway line it is almost certain that their three-quarters will pass back and back, and knock on inside their own 25. 6 (c). You might gain a penalty this way. 7 (a). The referee will then award a scrum for the knock-on and you will thus keep the ground you have gained.

SOME BOOKS TO READ

I am frequently asked for advice on what a Coarse Rugby player should read. Very little suitable is published, and most of that has been banned, but I would earnestly recommend *An Actor's Approach to his Part*, by Constantin Stanislavsky. The annual report of Watney Coombe and Reid is also interesting reading. For a good laugh I would suggest the Rugby Union Handbook, quite the funniest book ever written on the game. Why not read pieces to each other at half-time?

7

*. . . And in another minute there is a shout of "In Touch",
"Our Ball".'*—Tom Brown's Schooldays.

The enjoyment of Coarse Rugby depends to a
great extent upon the referee. The wrong sort
can ruin a game. Ideally, a referee should be
old, deaf or short-sighted, and fortunately a
great many are.

This can have its disadvantages. An old soul
who was resurrected for my Extra B had been
out of touch for so long that he kept awarding
four points for a drop goal. When we asked him
about the new Laws he looked puzzled and
said 'What new Laws?'

On the whole though, he was probably as
good as you'll get, although he did once award
a try without moving from the halfway line.
The sort who cannot be tolerated is the keen,
ambitious type who keeps giving little lectures
to the teams. Such men are dangerous.

'No, no, Vipers, you mustn't kick a man on
the ground when he hasn't got the ball. I

should award a penalty but this time I'll make it a scrum. Next time I shall be very angry indeed.'

It was a man of this sort who ordered me off the field because the nails in my boots were sticking out and told me to go into the road and scrape the nails down. A darn fool I looked standing in the middle of the Great West Road or thereabouts, scraping my feet and sending up showers of sparks. I felt like an old horse.

This type are always calling the two packs together and giving peace talks simply because they're trying underhand tricks to get the better of each other, just like a couple of international packs. And they always insist on playing thirty-five minutes each way (forty if they can get away with it) so that the game finishes in pitch darkness and icy cold, and there's only a couple of inches of muddy water in the bath and nothing for tea except crusts and a few cake crumbs. I'm not sure that referees of this sort haven't been responsible for the deaths of some delicate players as a result of a chill caught playing the full thirty-five minutes of the second half.

I remember a referee of this type controlling a game in which a hailstorm of great violence set in during the second half. Neither side had

scored and we slithered around rather aimlessly, getting colder and more miserable every
minute. Eventually the other team scored
about ten minutes from no-side. The kick was a
formality since the pitch was now so bad the
kicker could hardly stand.

As soon as the kick had failed we all marched
off the field, remembering to give three cheers
for our opponents, and dived for the bath. The
referee shouted for us to return, but we weren't
listening, so the other side walked off as well,
leaving the unfortunate ref bleating away in
the middle of the pitch like a lost lamb.

Apparently he was one of those heroes ob-
sessed by a sense of duty because he stood there
manfully until the full thirty-five minutes had
elapsed, whereupon he blew his whistle loud
and long (to the great interest of a small knot of
people under a tree who were fascinated by the
sight of a man standing by himself in the middle
of a rugby field during a hailstorm) and came
over to the dressing-room.

This particular side changed in a public-
house, the landlord of which provided a miserable trough with a little hot water in it. By the
time the ref arrived someone had pulled out the
plug and he had to wash himself in a puddle of
mud. Serve him right.

Funnily enough, the referees who live most in my memory are priests. Yes, priests. The first time I was refereed by a priest was at school when we played a Catholic college. I knew one of the boys on the other side, and when I heard him address the ref as 'Father' I presumed it was his own father, so I started calling him Mr. Smith.

He stuck it patiently for a time then took me aside and explained that he was not really Smith's father. I'm afraid that at that tender age I still didn't really grasp the relationship and I was under the delusion that he must be Mrs. Smith's second husband. But I stopped calling him Mr. Smith.

Then there was the time when the Extra B referee failed to arrive (a not infrequent occurrence) and our winger, a wild Irishman, produced another Irishman whom he said was a priest, and who would take charge.

Halfway through the game the Irishman went down groaning.

'Father,' he gasped to the referee, 'some bloody swine has kicked me in the groin.'

The priest winced. 'Hush, my son,' he said. 'Tell me who it was, and I will send the bastard off.'

As I said, he was an Irish priest.

We always seemed to be knocking up against priests and Irishmen in that club. One of our regular opponents was a sort of training college for priests (I don't think that is quite the correct title) and it was always the toughest game of the season.

The trouble with playing apprentice priests is that they do not smoke, because they are so poor, do not drink for much the same reason, and do not go out with women for obvious reasons. They are therefore supremely fit, with a lot of surplus energy to work off. When I add that their average was about twenty-two and they were nearly all Irish, you will see what I mean.

In contrast, our side had an average age of thirty. Everyone smoked like a chimney, drank like a drain and was highly uncelibate if they ever got the chance.

This game was *fierce*. No quarter was given or taken. The other side seemed to have a normal speed of twenty-five m.p.h. and to weigh sixteen stone. Soon tempers shortened, fists flew and the language got worse and worse.

We weren't the only offenders, by the way. There were some pretty un-priestlike statements flying around in the loose scrums I can tell you. But all the college words were what one might call secular swearing—that is, no blasphemy or obscenity. Just plain, honest oaths.

Eventually, after a particularly dirty piece of work in a maul, one of our forwards vented his feelings rather strongly.

The referee, who was a priest of course, blew a shrill blast.

'Penalty against Vipers,' he said.

'What for?' we asked sullenly.

'Blasphemy,' he replied firmly.

We lost.

Some of the team, who said they were strong non-Conformists, created a scene afterwards by hissing 'No Popery' when Grace was said before tea.

Luckily it passed off peaceably and we parted the best of friends, and swore that if ever we wanted to become priests we should go to that college.

On the whole, priests make good referees, because they seem to have a knack of control (I don't mean they necessarily make good Coarse Rugby referees, just good ordinary rugger referees). A priest was the only man who could control one side with a strong Irish element.

On Saturday nights, when they were at their

worst, the landlord used to ring the local priestery.

'For God's sake,' he would say somewhat untactfully, 'send over Father Flynn.' Probably a tankard would thud into the wall by his head as he was speaking.

Father Flynn simply walked in and said in one of those penetrating voices, 'Now then, lads, this has gone far enough.' All the Irishmen looked very sheepish and slunk away to the Irish Club where they could make as much noise as they liked.

Considering the importance I have laid on winning by any means it may seem strange that I have not mentioned the subject of bribing the referee, or providing one that doesn't need bribing.

The answer is simply that there's no *fun* in winning this way. It's too easy. Any fool can win if the ref's on his side. There's far more satisfaction to be gained by winning fairly and squarely by your own efforts (such as sending half the other side to the wrong ground).

In fact it's just not fair.

Of course, I have experienced games where the referee has been one-sided. A village club used to provide their own. He was a dreadful specimen, a great, fat, shaven-headed butcher with a stern determination that his side was going to win at all costs. For one thing, they were his customers. If an opponent dived over for a perfectly good try he instantly blew his whistle and there would be a long wait while he thought of an infringement. Sometimes he didn't even bother to think of an infringement, he just vaguely indicated a scrum somewhere near the 25 (defenders' ball, of course).

He awarded his own team a try if they grounded the ball anywhere within twenty yards of the opposition line.

He even shouted encouragement to his men during the game. You would be waiting to tackle a threequarter when the referee would appear, running beside him and shouting, 'Come on, Charlie, you've got them now. Never mind that bloke in front, you can beat him easily. . . .' It was difficult to decide which to tackle.

Good heavens, he once handed off a would-be tackler in his excitement. He picked a wrong 'un, because the player bounced back and tackled him savagely, but the damage was done.

This referee also had a habit of mysteriously getting in the way when our side were on the attack. Either a player ran into him or else he was in the way of the pass. Very strange.

No side had a fair chance of beating that village. What with a crooked touch-judge (I don't think we had more than two line-outs in the game), a crooked referee and about 150 crooked and violent spectators, the game was a farce. The beer was lousy, too.

Even the village policeman—a former player —did his bit. When we came out of the pub late on Saturday night, he was marching up and down, taking car numbers.

'These your vehicles, gentlemen?'

'Yes, you see we were playing in the match this afternoon . . .'

'I'm afraid I shall have to report you all for obstructing the 'ighway. This is a no-parking area.'

'But the other team said we could park here.'

'Yes,' he replied significantly. 'I don't doubt they did. And after watching the match this afternoon I don't blame them.'

As there are many splendid village clubs in Britain. I hasten to add that it's only one I'm writing of, not all of them.

No, it's too easy with a crooked referee. By all means try to secure a referee who is incompetent or open to persuasion, or so feeble that you can get away with anything. But don't pick a crook.

This, however, does *not* apply to touch-judges. If you are lucky enough to have one, you are perfectly entitled to expect him to be on your side. If the opposition provide one, you may be sure he will be on *their* side.

The touch-judge must not be too ostentatious in his support. It rather gives the game away if he cheers you on at the same time as giving a crooked decision.

Of course, he will favour you in his decisions. But there are other ways. He can, for instance, tap a spare ball on to the field in front of a forward rush. It causes no end of confusion among the pack. They all hunt around like hounds on a wrong scent.

Hissing, 'Quick—outside you,' as an enemy winger flashes along, can also be effective. He may pass the ball straight into touch.

But I do not agree with going so far as the touch-judge who simply dived on to the pitch and tackled a man as he was about to score. That is too obvious. By all means stick your flag between his legs, but please let us have some subtlety.

The sort of touch-judge who tackles a player is the founder, secretary and coach of a small district club. They keep up a running stream of invective and advice during the game, which is most unnerving, and often they cannot restrain themselves from rushing on to the field. A man of this type once threatened to knock my head off, and I spent the whole game in a misery of anticipation, because he was a huge man, but when no-side came he forgot all about it.

In a later match incidentally, he was actually sent off after rushing on the field, probably the only instance in the history of the game where a touch-judge has been sent off for obstruction.

Of all referees, the most irritating I have ever met was one with a son in the side. As soon as young Arthur joined the club he offered his service as referee to the coarse teams with the intention of keeping an eye on the young 'un.

'No, no, Arthur,' he used to say, wagging a finger. 'You really mustn't do that, son. You're supposed to roll away from the ball when you're tackled. You do see that, son, don't you? Here, let me show you. . . .'

Everyone was afraid to hurt young Arthur in front of his dad. He got away with murder. Whenever he scored—a not very frequent event —his father went berserk and capered around in delight. When he made a mess of things— which was much more frequently—his father stopped the game and showed him where he had gone wrong, while both teams stood round in the freezing cold.

But one must not be hard on referees. They have their little worries, just like human beings. It is not very pleasant to be handed three sets of false teeth during a game, although it is very funny when you give them back to the wrong people afterwards. One could almost write a chapter just on the adventures of false teeth handed to referees.

There was the referee who lost a set during a game, and he and the toothless owner spent two hours in complete darkness crawling round the pitch looking for them. They failed to find them, but during the week a girl, taking a short-cut across the field, came upon the gruesome objects lying in the grass and fled screaming.

In general, never hand anything to a referee to keep. I shall never forget a match when the ref had a hole in his pocket. After finding a gold watch trodden in the mud near the goal we abandoned the game and both teams went down on hands and knees scouring the pitch for valuables. We never did find some of them.

But we should be grateful to coarse referees. Remember, that whoever may be told about a cancelled fixture, it is never the referee. The secretary usually remembers that he hasn't told

. . . handed three sets of false teeth to keep.

the ref when he is doing his Saturday afternoon shopping, by which time the poor man is already changed and wondering where the teams are.

And coarse referees are capable of acts of great humanity.

When we were losing thirty-nil one of our veterans struggled over for his first try in five years. Unfortunately, he dropped the ball. The ref awarded a try.

'No,' he said afterwards, 'of course it wasn't a try, but if you'd seen the look on old Fred's face . . .'

8

'A chiel's amang you takin' notes, and faith he'll prent it.'
—Robert Burns.

It is the lot of coarse players to play for the most part under conditions of complete secrecy. As far as the world is concerned the players are utterly anonymous.

The trial of a new secret weapon is more public than the average coarse game. At least there will be the odd Russian spy lurking round the aerodrome disguised as a heap of old newspapers, but in Coarse Rugby the two teams conduct their epic battle unwatched by anyone except the referee (and sometimes without even him).

No one in his right senses will voluntarily watch a coarse match. Apart from the quality of the play, any spectator will be pressed into service as touch-judge on both sides of the field at once, asked to hold twenty-odd coats, watches and wallets, to cut up the lemons and serve them, and even to arbitrate disputes between the players. He is lucky if he is not asked to refcree or to play.

For this reason, Coarse Rugby teams are not recognised by the Press. No reporters attend their games. No headlines praise their dashing threequarters or blame their poor tackling.

Pictures of their mauls do not appear in the classy papers under such headings as:

AN AMUSING TUSSLE AT BLACKHEATH

Nor are the individual players featured thus:

TWICKENHAM FUDDY-DUDDIES SNUB JONES

or

RUGBY SNOBS BAN STAR WINGER

However, it is perhaps not quite accurate to say that the Press never reports the activities of Coarse Rugby players. After all, there is always this sort of thing in the local paper:

Found Crouching in the Bushes

RUGBY PLAYER'S ALLEGED THEFT

'Do You Know Who I Am'—*Alleged*

How a rugby player was found crouching in some bushes on St. Andrew's Park with a sign from a ladies' convenience concealed on him was described at Rottingham Magistrates' Court yesterday when the player, Frederick Fogg, of Mill Road, Bagford, was fined £10 for stealing the sign.

P.C. Ross said that as a result of a complaint he went to the convenience and found the sign missing. He saw Fogg trying to make off up an alley and gave chase. During the chase he was subjected to insults by other members of the team standing near their coach in the market square.

The P.C. alleged that when cornered,

Fogg said: 'You had better watch out, mate. Do you know who I am?'

The constable continued: 'I told him I did not know who he was, and Fogg replied: 'I am Sir Wavell Wakefield and all coppers are ———s. You had better watch out. I can make it pretty hot for you.''

Fogg also gave his address as c/o The Rugby Union, Twickenham, Middlesex. Enquiries revealed that this was not his correct address.

In court Fogg apologised, and said he had been playing for Bagford Vipers against Old Rottinghamians Extra B.

The chairman: The extra what?

Fogg: The Extra B.

Chairman: They seem a rather extraordinary Extra B to me (laughter).

'We lost 48-nil and that depressed me a little,' said Fogg. 'The next thing I knew was that I found myself with a lavatory sign in my hand.'

He denied he was drunk, and claimed he had only had two half-pints of beer. 'Normally I never drink on Saturday nights in the rugby season because I am always in strict training,' he said.

Fining Fogg, the chairman told him:

'This hooliganism must cease. I am going to make an example of you.'

Fogg was given time to pay.

Apart from such exhaustive reports as this, however, mention of Coarse Rugby is usually confined to a smudgy reference in the stop press column. This is phoned through by the captain of the winning side (the losing captain couldn't care less) and appears something like:

HOCKEY INTERNATIONAL
Old Rottinghamians Extra B 1, Bagford 2

RUGBY UNION
England 48 pts., Holland nil.

Sometimes the sports editor of the local paper allows teams to write their own reports. From these it would appear that the side has never deserved defeat and every try by the opposition has been an Act of God.

The only other occasion on which Coarse Rugby reaches the Press is a little paragraph in the local paper to the effect that the County Union have suspended Fred Fogg, of Bagford Vipers, following an incident in a recent game when thirteen players and the referee were injured.

They don't seem to print interesting news like that in these London papers. At home one could often find a juicy tit-bit of that type tucked away in the local Press, especially at the end of the season when players were becoming rather bored. It is not unknown for the evening paper to be intercepted and the offending passage removed before reaching the hands of the family.

News of this sort soon spreads. 'I see they got one of your team again. About time too, the dirty——' is a common saloon bar greeting.

Sometimes a player does not wish it to be known that he is playing. First-class clubs don't like their members turning out for minor mid-week games. Or he may even be trying to hide the fact from his wife. In this case a pseudonym is essential. There was a butcher in Leicester who used to play under the name of H. Bone, and another man in the team who appeared in the local paper as B. Jabers (he was Irish). Such little devices add a touch of the picturesque to the game.

However, all this is on a local level. Since the National Press will never report Coarse Rugby I feel it is my duty to do justice by publishing two reports, in which I shall say what the Press would say if it ever said it. The first report is how a popular newspaper might report a game:

VETERAN FRED IS MATCH HERO

O. Rottinghamians Extra B o, Bagford Vipers B 3 pts.

Hey nonny-no! What a smiling breakfast it was this morning for 41-year-old railway clerk, Fred Fogg, veteran pack leader of Bagford Vipers third team. Never had the toast been crisper as he sat in the parlour of his little terraced house near the canal . . . never had the coffee been tastier . . . never had the bacon been nicer, the eggs better cooked.

REASON?

On Saturday burly Fred (he admits to weighing 17 stone) scored the only try of the game, which gave Bagford Vipers B their first win for three seasons.

Not only that *but it was Fred's first try for 18 years!*

'I remember my last try well,' he said excitedly after the game, as he poured a tot of rum into his shandy. 'It was just before the Battle of El Alamein I wrote home to tell the wife about it.'

No wonder both spectators cheered him to the echo as he left the field!

Fred said he had been in special training for the game, because he was determined to score before the season ended.

'Yes,' he said, 'I gave up Bass at the start of the week and drank only the local mild. Rugby is a game you've got to take seriously.'

Fred's try came near the end of the game, after as grim a duel as could be imagined on the dark mud of the Old Rottinghamians' spare pitch at Cow Field.

Riddle of Winger

A scrum was ordered 15 yards from the Old Boys' line. The two packs met . . . and no one noticed that Fred was still talking to the Bagford secretary, who was touch-judge, at the side of the field. In any case, Bagford had only *four forwards*.

Yet by a terrific effort they heeled and diminutive sixteen-year-old Mike Smith, their scrum-half, whipped out the ball on the blind side.

Then he realised to his horror there was no winger! Vipers were so short of men he had gone into the pack!

The ball lay stuck in the mud. THEN FRED TOOK A HAND.

Attracted by the shouting on the pitch he turned round from his conversation with the touch-judge and saw the ball. In a flash he had picked it up and lumbered over the Old Rottinghamians' line for the winning try.

The Old Boys protested strongly, but the referee insisted that Fred was within the Laws. As if to add emphasis to his ruling the conversion kick hit a post and brought down the crossbar, knocking out five Old Rottinghamians.

I SAY that the diehard, stick-in-the-mud England selectors should carefully note the name of Fred Fogg.

I SAY that despite his age, Fred shows a resourcefulness that is sadly lacking in the present England pack.

***See *Shoot Twickenham Tyrants—Page Six*

So much for the popular papers. The classy Press, however, would treat the whole affair much differently. Something like this:

A PUZZLING INCIDENT
AT COW FIELD

DISPUTE OVER TRY
By Our Own Correspondent
O. Rottinghamians Extra B 0 pts., Bagford
Vipers B 3 pts.

The Duke of Wellington is reported by
historians to have said during the Battle of
Waterloo (or was it Badajoz?): 'This is
hard pounding, gentlemen, we shall see
who can pound the longest.'

But for the fact that he died in 1852, it
would have been interesting to have had
the Iron Duke's comments on the game at
Cow Field between these two old rivals.
One feels he would have said much the
same thing.

The match did not begin propitiously.
Cow Field steamed dankly in the drizzle
as the two sides walked on, some 55 minutes after the advertised time of kick-off,
and a count of heads soon showed that the
Old Boys had twelve players to the Vipers'
eleven, one of whom had never played
rugby before.

Winning the toss, Old Rottinghamians elected to kick down the considerable slope (almost one-in-five in parts of the field) and were soon on the attack. Unfortunately, owing to the drizzle and the slope the two teams were almost invisible in the far corner and spectators could judge the progress of events only by a faint baying sound, like hounds at the scent, which occasionally issued forth, indicating that some move or other was in progress.

A Lamentable Kick

However, after a quarter of an hour, Owen, the Vipers' stand-off, emerged up the hill with the ball and fell flat on his face. He refused to release the ball, despite the earnest adjurements of several opponents, who reinforced their arguments with their boots. and a penalty was awarded against Vipers. This was the first incident of note in the game.

The penalty was not in an impossible position, being some 20 yards out and dead in front of the posts, but the ball travelled only six feet before coming to rest in the mud.

Vipers were definitely hampered by being four men short, but the numerical deficiency was lessened when the Old Boys' inside centre left the field, apparently after an altercation with his captain over his habit of running round in circles with the ball. He appeared to be uninjured, but refused to return, despite shouts from the field.

By now the pitch was waterlogged with the continual rain and Williams, the Vipers' second-row and wing forward combined, had bad luck when he sank up to his ankles just in front of the Old Boys' goal, and was unable to move. Later this player left the field for a short spell, saying he was exhausted with the effort.

One must query certain tactics of the Vipers. Was it necessary, for instance, to kick the ball into the nearby canal so frequently? Each time this resulted in a delay of ten minutes while the ball was recovered in a punt, which subsequently sank at its moorings under mysterious circumstances, causing even more delay. This occurred after a Vipers' player had gone to retrieve the ball.

A Noteworthy Tactic

However, the move in which the Vipers formed a solid circle around the man with the ball and marched down the field, crushing all opposition, was reminiscent of the tactics employed by the late I. (Hackers) Smith-Brown, the famous captain of Old Snobfordians in their heyday before the First World War. One wonders how Vipers came to hear of this scheme, for the move has fallen into disuse recently. Surely the shade of the great Smith-Brown was hovering over them.

In this connection it is worth remembering that Smith-Brown, as his nickname implies, fought for years for the retention of hacking in the last century, and was associated with Blackheath in the famous schism over this. If he had seen this game he would have been happy to see that whatever the rules may say, hacking is by no means a dead letter.

And so the struggle continued until half-time, when Old Rottinghamians were strengthened by the return of their centre, who was greeted with a shower of orange peel.

After the interval things waxed even more furious. As Tennyson might have commented, 'And all day long the noise of battle rolled. . . .' Yet the only score of the match did not come until a few minutes from no-side.

An Unusual Occurrence

The exact circumstances were not clear. A scrum formed not far from the Old Rottinghamians' line and the ball was passed out on the blind side by the Vipers' scrum-half. As there was no winger (that individual having gone into the scrum, owing to the shortage of players), the ball lay in the mud for several seconds. The next thing that became clear was that F. Fogg, one of the Vipers' forwards, was plunging unopposed over the line.

The whole affair was obscured by mist, drizzle and darkness. Fogg said that he had been talking to the touch-judge, but that he had not left the field of play, nor had he advanced in front of the ball.

The Old Rottinghamians, however, vehemently claimed that Fogg had left the field to answer a call of nature, and had rushed back on from behind a nearby tree, to seize the ball and score the winning try.

One would have thought that the touch-judge could have solved the problem, but he remained mute throughout the entire proceeding.

Even so, it would be churlish to detract from Vipers' victory. If they cannot say with Henry V, 'To God be the glory,' they can at least echo the words of Wellington at the Battle of Waterloo (or was it Badajoz?), 'It was a damn'd close run thing . . .'

I apologise if parts of the above fantasy are somewhat obscure to coarse players. The Duke of Wellington was a famous general. Tennyson was a well-known poet, and Henry the Fifth was a play written by Shakespeare, who was a not inconsiderable playwright at one time. They all lived long ago, but people go around quoting bits of what they used to say, chiefly to show how clever they are and because they can't think of anything as good themselves.

The incident of the player talking to the touch-judge and then running on to score is quite true. It happened in 1951 when Stoneygate Second XV were playing Notts. Tigers in a field six miles from the nearest habitation. I should know, because I was the Stoneygate scrum-half, and I have never been so surprised as when one of our second-row galloped up on the blind side.

Finally, a word of practical advice in connection with the Press. If you *are* ever caught with a lavatory sign up your sleeve, don't offer the reporter at court half-a-crown to keep the case out of the paper. He certainly will not keep it out—and he may even take the half-crown.

9

'Then there's fuddling about in the public-house, and drinking bad spirits and punch, and such rot-gut stuff. That won't make drop-kicks or chargers of you, take my word for it . . .'—Tom Brown's Schooldays.

Some of a rugby player's happiest memories concern the social side—particularly away games and tours. Strictly speaking, these are activities not confined by any means to the coarse side of the game, but I always feel that a coarse player shines best under such circumstances.

The lower the playing ability, the more noise and damage a team will make. The First XV may create a disturbance in an hotel, but the Extra B will wreck the place. One reason is that the lower sides tend to attract the more emotionally unstable element, the misfits in life as in rugby.

Having nothing better to do at full-back, I considered a coarse team once as they moved aimlessly from side to side of the pitch in front of me, neither making nor giving ground. The

side included a man with a gaol record; a man
suspended from driving; another whose wife
was divorcing him for coming home tight and
hitting her with a kettle; two Irishmen dodging
their income-tax by moving from building site
to building site; a neurotic with a twitch, fresh
from hospital; and an unemployable layabout.
The rest (there were only about four of them)
seemed fairly normal, but one never knows.

As far as I could see, the other team were
little better. They had a strange, moon-faced
creature called Charlie with one of those dreadful vacant laughs beloved by horror film pro-
ducers. This laugh was produced whenever
something unpleasant happened, such as when
a player was injured. 'Hur—hur—hur' it went,
sending shivers up my spine.

In the First XV, if a player fails to turn up,
there is a long inquest and a stern phone call
next day. A Coarse Rugby captain knows a
phone call is useless. Frequently the reply goes,
'So you want to talk to Mr. Flynn as to why he
didn't play rugby yesterday? And 'tis meself
that would like to know where Mr. Flynn is,
for hasn't he fled the house yesterday taking all
his luggage and owing me six weeks' rent? And
what I want to know is why those two policemen came to the house this afternoon, asking

after him? And this a respectable neighbour-hood and him saying that he'd paid all the instalments on the radio . . .'

It is sometimes necessary to make a rule that the club is not responsible for debts and rent arrears incurred by such players. In the absence of their tenant, landladies have been known to seek justice with the club, even to screeching insults and abuse from the touch-line.

Every coarse side has at least one inveterate exhibitionist. They can be an embarrassment at times, like the player who insisted on changing in a Tube train because his side were late for a game. When the team reached their destination he was only half-changed and made a great show of going up the escalator almost naked.

This particular player had a beard. I don't trust bearded players (although I wore a beard myself for a few months, and darn fool I must have looked, too). If there is any dirty work going on among the other side, look out for old beardy. You know what to do.

I can never understand why hotel landlords accept rugby clubs as guests at all. They spend all the time in a state of siege and hysteria, listening with growing anxiety to the distant noise of obscene singing, varied with a scream from the female guest who has discovered a drunken front-row forward in the ladies' toilet.

One can only suppose that they have no idea what they are letting themselves in for. Sometimes they react strongly when they discover. Many a team has had to move after the first night. Often they leave with an air of righteous indignation, telling the landlord that if he doesn't want their custom, there are plenty of places which do. They reckon without the grapevine. Sometimes the same team arrive back penitent the same night, begging for shelter, as no one else will have them.

If the landlord is stupid he takes them in again, and within five minutes they are as bad as ever.

No one blames the landlord. After all, when a player is locked in a wardrobe which topples over, and then kicks his way out of the back, what can you expect?

In fairness, though, it must be said that rugby teams are often their own victims. A player whose car would not start borrowed a friend's from the hotel yard and, on returning in the early hours, parked so clumsily as to damage his own car severely. When he came down to breakfast with a splitting headache, another guest said: 'Some idiot was crashing about the car park last night and banged into your car.'

'I know,' said the player dismally.

'Don't worry,' cried the guest triumphantly. *'I got his number.'*

During any tour the team psychopaths—and there are usually about six of them—must be closely watched and if necessary guarded. It may be wiser to leave them behind. These are the louts who in recent years have spoiled things for everyone by breaking out into orgies of wanton damage and theft.

In the old days any damage was at least accidental and paid for immediately. If a glass was broken it was because a player was trying to balance it on his head, not because he threw it to the floor with a childish laugh, like the West Bar cowboys at Twickenham. And our goings-on did have some originality, if of a rather macabre kind.

Looking back on some of the incidents, it is difficult to believe they ever happened. Can it be true, for instance, that a team once moved all the lamps from a hole in the road and strung them across the main street of Cardiff, stopping all the traffic?

It seems equally incredible that we once kidnapped a passer-by and drove him away in the coach. We were merely digging up the name-board of the opponents' ground before leaving when a respectable citizen on a cycle upbraided us. In a twinkling he was in the coach—complete with bicycle—and being driven out of town. I cannot think why he did not sue. Perhaps the whole thing seemed just a horrid hallucination after we had let him go.

Strangely enough, the higher up the social scale, the worse the behaviour becomes.

It was a sales manager who emptied a dust-bin over the hotel banisters on a group of singing players.

It was a doctor who switched the signs on the Ladies' and Gents' conveniences, with consequent embarrassment and discomfiture all round.

And it was a headmaster who secured an article of female attire and flew it from a hotel flagpole.

Of course all this sort of thing is most jolly until it happens to *you*. Then it's a very different matter. I have known clubs which boasted of their exploits on tour, and whose pavilions were filled with souvenirs such as No Parking signs, who became furious if anyone stole something of theirs, or began to break up the bar.

A team I was with became boisterous and

hid a car by pushing it into some bushes. This tickled us so much that we went back into the bar roaring with laughter, and invited the other side to join us in the joke.

'You'll never guess,' we howled, 'we've just

'We've just pushed some chap's Austin Seven into the bushes . . .'

got some chap's old Austin Seven and we've pushed it right in among those bushes! He'll never be able to find it!'

Suddenly one of the opposition went white. 'I don't think that's funny,' he said stiffly. 'You'll hear more of this.'

He walked out and started searching among the bushes, so we could guess why he was so annoyed. But the funny thing was that only half an hour before he'd been boasting of his exploits in snatching souvenirs on tour.

I may say he had considerable difficulty in getting his car out of the bushes, because no one would help him.

I believe that was the evening on which we had an extraordinary game of darts on the way home, in which arrows were flying all over the saloon bar and the customers were ducking for their lives. It was only justice that one of our own men walked in front of the board while they were throwing and was nearly pinned to the wall by a dart through his ear. No praise can be too high for the forbearance of coach drivers on trips like this. They maintain complete calm, even on such occasions as when half the coach wanted the sliding roof closed and half desired it open. The battle only ended when someone found himself on top of the roof, with the hatch shut. For a moment we couldn't think where he was until we heard a plaintive knocking from above. The silly idiot was sitting on the hatch when we slid it back to let him in, and he nearly shot off the back of the coach.

Some of the coarsest rugby I have ever played was in the Services. By Service rugby I don't mean the sort they play at Twickenham, which perpetuates the myth that anyone in or out of the Services really cares whether the Army beat the Navy. No, I mean the real Service rugby, in which the Bullshires turn out one short because the full-back is doing jankers for failing to polish the soles on his spare pair of boots.

The main thing which distinguishes Service rugby from any other section of the game is that two-thirds of the team don't mix with the others after the game. This is because Queen's Regulations specify dreadful punishments for officers and men found carousing together. Things may be different now, but I can't say the officers exactly made much effort to improve this situation, at least not when I was a spotty-faced young trooper of seventeen. The four or five other ranks arrived at the ground in a three-tonner (usually the coal-truck for some reason). The officers arrived in jeeps. We played our game. The officers vanished immediately it was over and we did not see them again. If it was an away game we were, however, invited to partake of a meal, apparently composed of sawdust, in the nearest cookhouse.

This situation reaches the height of absurdity when there is only one ranker in the side and he solemnly troops off to have tea by himself. A former Eastern Counties' threequarter told me that when this happened to him, he was allowed to have tea with the others but had to sit at a separate table. Unfortunately, he upset a cup of tea all over the tablecloth, which rather weakened his case for equal treatment.*

Sometimes, however, the boot is on the other foot. I always felt sorry for the only officer in the regiment's soccer side. The rest of the team used to gather in a corner of the dressing-room as far away as possible, and mutter at him.

But there is one good thing about Service rugger—it does occasionally give an opportunity to pay off old scores. Not for nothing, certain N.C.O.s seem reluctant to play. One unpopular skipper, a humourless lieutenant, made the mistake of holding a trial match which

* This was in the 'forties. I believe things have changed since then.

Service rugger gives an opportunity to pay off old scores

developed into a positive brawl as various
grudges were settled. The rankers had nothing
to lose. The skipper *had* to select all the officers

first or his life would not have been worth living.

The unfortunate adjutant, a much-misunderstood man, was the chief target of an ape-like Rugby League player who had recently returned from a field punishment centre, whence the adjutant had been instrumental in consigning him. He was kicked so hard on the knee that he walked with a stick for three months. The League player was mysteriously posted.

They did not hold another trial game, but continued to pick the team in descending order of rank.

Yet Service rugger is not entirely a wasted experience. It can provide a soldier with the greatest boon by enabling him to miss guard mounting. And anything that does that cannot be completely worthless.

'Penalty try? We don't have them in this valley, ref'—
Dai Evans.

One of the greatest centres of Coarse Rugby is
Wales, although it is a special form of the game,
adapted to suit their own native talents and
genius.

My first contact with the Welsh was as a
small child, sitting with my parents in the members' stand at Welford Road, Leicester. I recall
my father going purple in the face and I asked
'Mummy, why is Daddy waving his fist at that
man in the white shirt?' Mother gently replied,
'Because he's a Swansea player, dear.'

Since then I have discovered more about
Welsh rugby. I am also able to appreciate why
father was waving his fist.

Coarse Rugby in Wales is played in two
forms. There is a version played by small teams
in the towns, and the Welsh version, played by
village sides in the valleys of Monmouth,
Glamorgan and Carmarthen. The distinction

between the two is that the first version is mark-
ed by the chief characteristic of English Coarse
Rugby—a casual approach to the game.
Valley rugby, however, although coarse in the
best sense of the word is approached with a
religious fervour (not for nothing are rugby
posts known as the altars of Wales. There are
as many rugby pitches as chapels). Indeed,
during the grim years of depression, although
the mine might be deserted and the steelworks
rusting, the rugby field would still be carefully
looked after and the sacred rites performed
every Saturday, even if the team could scarcely
raise twopence between them.

Incidentally, do not refer to Monmouth as
part of England. The Act of Union of 1536
does not exist as far as Welsh rugby circles are
concerned.

This tradition of religious fervour can be a
burden. A Welshman is expected to have an
encyclopaedic knowledge of the game, even if
he has no interest in it. If he professes ignorance
outside Wales his listeners won't even believe he
is a real Welshman at all. As English rugby
suffers from the myth of the invisible Union
Jack flying over the scrum, so Welsh Coarse
Rugby suffers from the religious fetish, fostered
by those epic mining novels in which sin, guilt

and sex march hand in hand and all the leading
characters are carried in dead at the end.

This sort of thing:

'And everyone is shouting now, and there is
Maldwyn the tallyman, the blue scar showing
on his arm, about to throw the ball, and there
on the touchline is Blodwen, with her ripe
cherry lips parted and her big bosom heaving,
and Dai thinks how soft and warm she is when
he kisses her behind the coal-tip, and almost
forgets the game. But see, Maldwyn has thrown
in true, and Ianto, the shot-firer, has it and
hurls it back to Rhys the winding-gear engineer,
who dodges round the front of the line-out and
now the ball is in Dai's arms, as cosy and safe
as ever Blodwen nestled there, and all is a
roaring, like when there is a roof-fall in the pits
and there is Dai's old Da weeping for joy and
crying to Heaven as his son dives over for the
winning try . . .'

It is very difficult in real life to live up to that
sort of thing, even for a Welshman. And only a
Welsh writer could mix sex and rugby like that.

Times have changed in the valleys as everywhere else. People used to talk about valley
rugby as if the people who played it belonged to
some savage tribe with cannibal rites.

Actually there may have been some truth in

this sort of thing if one can go by the experience of a friend who worked in South Wales. He rashly volunteered to play for the local village, thinking he might have a gentle run-out with the third team.

Unfortunately there was no third team, or second team either. To make matters worse he was a schoolmaster and stand-off, and Welsh have a great respect for both breeds.

'Can't leave out an educated man like that,' said the selection committee and picked him for the hardest game of the season, against the village 'over the hill'.

Word filtered to the other village that their enemies had a new stand-off ('Educated man, too, they say') and plans were laid to flatten him.

My friend was a gentle creature, just about fitted for the third team of a London Old Boys' side, and he suffered terribly at the hands of a huge wing forward who wasn't particularly shoosey whether he had the ball or not. At one point, he said, he even considered running away.

When the game finished the wing forward approached my friend, his arm outstretched to shake hands. But by this time the stand-off was in such a state of nerves that he imagined the man wanted to hit him and he fled from the field, never to play again.

Most coarse Welsh teams seem to breed a special type of human being, usually a prop forward. He is distinguished physically by having no neck, the head (which is shaved) being attached direct to the spine. The specimen weighs sixteen stone and when it stands erect (which is not very often) is 5 ft. 9 in. tall. The arms reach to the knees, the locomotion is by means of a typical shambling, ape-like gait.

Such men are apparently born—or hewn— at the age of thirty and stay the same age for fifteen years, when they suddenly grow old overnight, give up the game and sit wearing their mufflers in the Welfare, telling everyone about the great days of long ago.

The hooker is of a special breed, too. He is always in his mid-thirties, bald, and without any teeth. On the touch-line stands a replica of the hooker. The two are indistinguishable. This is his father, who used to hook for the same side. The father will be holding the hand of a small infant, whose hair is already receding and who has bad teeth. That is his grandson. In twenty years he, too, will hook for the village. By then he will be bald and will have no teeth.

Welsh sides are renowned for the vigour of their

A special type of human being . . .

forward play ('Never mind the ball, get on with the game'). In this they are inspired by the Legend of the Terrible Eight. No one really knows who the original Terrible Eight were. Some say they belonged to Newport, others

that they belonged to Wales. But the legend
has grown so misty now that many village sides
believe it was *their* pack which was the Terrible
Eight and they must keep up the tradition. Behind the scrum are seven men all looking
exactly alike, except for slight variations in
height. They are all dark and wiry and have
tenor voices (whoever heard of a baritone in
the backs?).

There is another remarkable thing about the
backs. They have all won a schoolboy international cap for Wales. If all the Welshmen
who claimed to have a schoolboy cap were
added up, there woud be enough to turn out a
different schoolboy international side every
week for thirty years. In fact I don't think I've
ever met a Welshman who hasn't had at least
a trial for the national schools' team. I should
like to know how they pick these schoolboy
sides. Do they choose them in batches of 100
and play 50 a-side?

Many of the team will be related, and whole
families may be playing together. They say
there used to be a complete family pack of
seven brothers and their father before the war.
Possibly some player will have only one arm.
In Wales they don't let a matter like the loss of a
limb stop them from playing rugby, even if it

stops them from working. One-armed men are incredibly adept in the line-outs, scooping the ball back with great accuracy. They are also most difficult to tackle, as they defend themselves by thrusting their hips at the attacker.

It is almost certain that an aged committee member will be playing. There is always one who secretly believes he is as good as he ever was, and who happens to bring along his kit in case anyone fails to turn up. I suspect such men of bribing players to feign sickness, so that they can live their years of glory again.

The pitch is on a hillside, with a slope of one in seven. Because of this, play tends to be confined to a bog in one corner, a fact which accounts for the development and importance of the human cannonballs in the pack described earlier. It is said that some Welsh valley forwards develop a leg which is shorter than the other through constant scrummaging on a slope.

There will be a good turn-out of spectators, vehement, knowledgeable and partisan. They will include several sheep and the inevitable dog, but not many women. The valleys are spared the distracting female squeaking* that

* *Not you, dear.*

accompanies English rugby, even at the coarse level.

Among the crowd may well be a Rugby League scout. Technically he shouldn't even be allowed on the ground, but as he is probably related to the President, he can't very well be turned away. Besides, nobody wants to turn him away. Who knows but that he may approach a player after the game with a tempting offer to go North?

It is not necessarily the ambition of every Welsh player to go North, but it is certainly his ambition to be able to say he refused an offer. It is an honour second only to receiving an international cap. At least one player from the village will have made his name in the League, and have an honoured place in the club's history, even though officially he is a pariah. The religious myth takes a knock here, as people do not normally change their religion because someone starts waving five-pound notes around. But then, rugby is the only religion in which one is actually bribed to leave the faithful. It is lucky some obscure American sect has not thought of the idea and started to send scouts round the valley chapels, picking out the best tenors.

The dressing-room may be a corrugated iron

hut and sanitation non-existent. If there is a lavatory, the door will be designed so that it can be taken off easily and used as a stretcher. I knew a club which used to carry hot water up the hillside in buckets for a bath. There were three big wooden tubs for washing in after the game. In the first players were allowed to wash only their feet, in the next their arms and faces and the third tub was reserved for their torsos.

In this village an unusual rite took place after the game, when everyone ate raw kippers, to enable them to have a big enough thirst to tackle that revolting flat beer which Welshmen seem to like so much.

The beer was drunk in a little pub kept by a man who claimed to be an old international. I hear there was once a pub in Wales which *wasn't* kept by an old cap, but all the trade dropped off and they gave up the licence.

THE CAP was framed behind the bar. At least, the landlord said it was his cap, but he seemed remarkably vague about the exact year in which he played, and in what position. In fact he didn't really seem to know much about it at all.

'At Twickenham it was,' he said. 'Before the war. No, I dunno which war you mean, I mean

the war. There was Willy Jones outside me and
Dai Jones inside me . . . what position? Ful-
back, of course, I told you before. The crowd
went mad when I scored. Threw their bagpipes
in the air and jumped on their kilts . . . yes, of
course it was at Twickenham, I told you
so . . .'

Personally I think the man was a fraud.

Later that night, the singing began. Only
one player on the home side could not sing like
an opera star, and he played the spoons. He
confided that all his life he had felt inferior because he was tone-deaf and whoever heard of a
tone-deaf Welshman? (Once again, the Welsh
are trapped by their own tradition.)

Then his old Da, a grand man, who used to
play for the village, taught him to play the
spoons, and within a few weeks he was the most
popular man in the side.

And deservedly, too. He was the only man I
know who could play the accompaniment to
'The Day Thou Gavest Lord Is Ended' on two
teaspoons. I commend the idea to Church
authorities everywhere.

The early part of the evening was given over
to low songs, but about 9.30 they went on to
hymns. Only the Welsh could follow an un-
printable bellow with the 23rd Psalm. This was

duly rendered with spoon obbligato, and we finished, traditionally, with Cwm Rhondda (spoon solo between verses and accompaniment on beer tumblers).

It was a good night. Perhaps those mining novelists have the right idea after all.

'Give 'im a letter, can't do no better . . .'—Kipling.

OLD ROTTINGHAMIANS R.F.C.
Affiliated to the Rugby Union
Founded 1925

Patron:

THE MAYOR OF
ROTTINGHAM

Ground: Whiteacre Road,
Rottingham.
(Buses 19, 22 from Central
Station to Oak Lane, walk
down lane for half-mile,
turn left over stile, then
right by electricity pylon,
ground is 500 yards on left
down cinder path.)

The Secretary,
Bagford Vipers F.C.,
8, Gas Street,
Bagford.

Dear Sir,

      I am instructed by my committee to

write to you in protest over certain incidents in the match last Saturday between our Extra B and your B side.

The first matter concerns an incident in which a Vipers' player referred to one of our team, who is a coloured gentleman, as a nigger and said: 'Get off my head or it will be the worse for you. I shall get out my white sheet and tar and feather you.'

I may add that the player in question is an Old Boy of the School and a Paramount Chief of the Oozongo tribe, British Somaliland. After completing his education in this country he will return there to take up his duties as Chief and the Colonial Office take an extremely serious view of this insult.

Secondly, we wish to protest concerning the behaviour of the Vipers' touch-judge, who, I am informed, persistently shouted abuse and threats at our team while carrying out his duties in a somewhat partisan manner and who was eventually ordered from the field by the referee. He then entered the bar and caused considerable distress to our lady members by using obscene and insulting language.

Thirdly, there is the matter of our flagpole, which vanished from the ground at about the same time your coach left. From various evidence we have reason to believe that it was removed in the Vipers' coach and we should appreciate the earliest return of this flagpole, in good condition, and with flag, otherwise we shall be obliged to charge you for same.

Fourthly, we should like to clarify the result of the game for our records. Our captain informs us that with the score at 55-nil in the favour of Old Rottinghamians, your side walked off the field in protest at the dismissal of the touch-judge, and that you are now claiming the match was abandoned as a draw.

We should like to state that in our opinion it would have been physically impossible for you to have scored 55 points in the remaining ten minutes.

Fifthly, we note with regret that after your side had ordered 48 hot dogs from the bar at 9d. each, a sum of only 3½d. was forthcoming. This leaves a deficiency of £1 15s. 8½d., which we should be glad to receive at your convenience.

One of our committee members complains that while he was in the bar his car was pushed into the pond in the next field by members of your team and he asks your co-operation in finding the malefactors and charging for the cost of a tow out of the pond.

We also have to ask you for payment for the pavilion door, which was totally destroyed by your members.

During the evening fifty-six glasses were broken, and we suggest you pay for half of these at 2s. each.

I look forward to receiving your observations on these matters.

Yours faithfully,

L. SYMINGTON-SMITH,

Hon. Secretary.

BAGFORD VIPERS F.C. (Rugby Union)
Founded 1886

Ground: Eastern Park,
Bagford.

L. Smyington-Smith Esq.,
Secretary
Old Rottinghamians R.F.C.
Whiteacre Road,
Rottingham.

Dear Sir,

We have received your letter with. if I may say so, amazement. How anyone could be so childish passes our comprehension. As regards this bloke who says he was called a nigger and, etc., well, what can you expect, because we have a centre threequarter called Rossetti, who is of Italian extraction, and one of your players, I don't know who, but it was a nasty greasy little bloke, he called him a Wog and later made an insulting reference about Mussolini which upset our man I can tell you, seeing that he has been naturalised for many years

I cannot comment on the referee's dastardly action in sending off the touch-judge because I was the touch-judge, but I may say in passing that he won't ever ref one of our games again and we have never seen such a one-sided referee, where did you get him, off the local refuse dump? It wouldn't have been 55-nil, it wouldn't have been 5-nil with a decent referee so we are right in claiming a draw, and anyway it is going down in our records as a draw.

I don't know about this tea money you say we owe, but I do know this and that is that we bought twice as much beer as you, and you must have at least thirty bob left in the beer kitty which you didn't spend, as our chaps say they couldn't get a drink out of you all night, so if you are going to be niggly over a few bob then you can send back the beer kitty what was left over.

Not that the beer was any good, why don't you get them to put in draught Bass, our chaps won't drink anything else, it was like gnat's water what we had

Then this flagpole. I may tell you it is libel to go round saying we stole it and you can get put into court for saying things like that. We don't know anything about your rotten flagpole, all I will say is if you look on that bit of waste ground at the back of the gasworks you may find something to your advantage. I make this statement without prejudice.

That car you say we shoved into the pond, well, half of them were your chaps and they thought it a great joke because they didn't like the owner, so I suggest you put your own nest in order before you start bolting the door after the bird has flown.

It was the same with that door, all our blokes wanted to do was to take it off its hinges and one of your men put his foot through the glass first, I know because my son, Fred, saw it all.

I have personal experience of seeing the glasses broken, who suggested singing 'The Muffin Man' anyway, it was your lot, wasn't it? so what are you moaning about, eh?

In conclusion, all I can say is that the committee were very annoyed by your letter and

we feel you ought to show a bit more of the
spirit of the rugby game, not that one can
expect it from an old boys' club. I always say
the old boys are killing rugby by keeping
promising youngsters from older clubs in the
district, I said as much at the county committee
last week and I notice you weren't there.

> Yours truly,
> ALFRED FOGG,
>> *Secretary.*

The Secretary,
Bagford Vipers F.C.,
8, Gas Street,
Bagford.

Dear Sir,

I want to apply to join your club as a playing
member. I am an Old Rottinghamian and have
played for the Old Boys, chiefly in the Extra B
for the last two seasons, but they are a rotten
lot and they never give me a chance in a better
side. I met your blokes the other week and they
seemed very decent. I play wing-forward,
stand-off or scrum-half. I am 18.

I look forward to receiving a quick reply.

> Yours, etc.,
> ARTHUR SYMINGTON-SMITH.

Extract from minutes of Bagford Vipers F.C. (Rugby Union):

'IT WAS RESOLVED that the application of A. Symington-Smith for membership be approved, subject to clearance from Old Rottinghamians.'

OLD ROTTINGHAMIANS R.F.C.
Affiliated to the Rugby Union
Founded 1925

Patron:
THE MAYOR OF
ROTTINGHAM

Ground: Whiteacre Road, Rottingham.
(Buses 19, 22 from Central Station to Oak Lane, walk down lane for half-mile, turn left over stile, then right by electricity pylon, ground is 500 yards on left down cinder path.)

The Secretary,
Bagford Vipers F.C.,
8, Gas Street,
Bagford.

Dear Sir,
    I am instructed by my committee to say we are appalled at your action over Mr. Arthur

Symington-Smith, who happens to be my son. My committee feel that this deliberate poaching of our younger players is the last straw, following the disgraceful scene at our ground and your unsatisfactory reply.

In view of this and the previous matter I have to inform you that my committee has decided to cancel all future fixtures between our two clubs.

Yours faithfully,
L. SYMINGTON-SMITH,
Hon. Secretary.

P.S. I have told Arthur he is not to play for you.

Note left beside telephone of the secretary of the local fixtures exchange some months later:

JACK: THE VIPERS RANG, AND THEY HAD FORGOTTEN THAT SATURDAY'S FIXTURE WAS CANCELLED. CAN YOU FIX THEIR 'B' UP WITH A GAME AT HOME, PREFERABLY NO ONE TOO STRONG.——MAGGIE. P.S. YOUR DINNER IS IN THE OVEN.

Extract from the Bagford Evening Monitor *on the following Friday:*

RUGBY UNION

Additional fixture:

Eastern Park (3 p.m.): Bagford Vipers 'B' *v.*
Old Rottinghamians Extra B.

THE ART OF COARSE DRINKING
Michael Green

The Coarse Drinker:
A man who blames his hangover on the tonic and not the gin.
A man who looks at the wine list first, chooses the booze, and then picks the food to go with it.
A man who needs no coy excuse – he needs a drink because he needs a drink.

Do you know the difference in licensing hours between Gloucester and Sheringham during the summer?
After a party have you ever sneaked round all the half empty glasses and finished them off?
Is Capital Punishment justified in the case of a person who fails to buy his round?

If the answer to these questions is yes you are almost certainly a Coarse Drinker.

THE ART OF COARSE SAILING

Michael Green

The Coarse Sailor:
One who in a crisis forgets nautical language and shouts, 'For God's sake turn left'.
One whose sailing history includes having put his boom through the window of a grocer's shop.

'With a shout of 'Boyur', *Quiet Dawn* turned into wind in the middle of the river and started to drift sideways towards the railway bridge at an alarming rate . . . Meanwhile Dennis was trying to restore steerage way by rowing with the quant pressed against the mast, looking rather like an ancient Phoenician oarsman. Arthur was pumping the tiller to bring the bows round and shouting at Joan to start paddling with the deck mop.'

If you have ever witnessed a scene like this, you were watching coarse sailors in action.

THE ART OF COARSE GOLF

Michael Green

The Coarse Golfer:
One who when playing alone, is regularly overtaken by women's foursomes.
One who normally goes from tee to green without touching the fairway.
One who has to shout "Fore" when he putts.

A lonely man, the Coarse Golfer. Separated not only from other golfers, but from the golf course as well. A trail of divots leading into a thicket. The sound of cursing and thrashing from afar. Somewhere out there the Coarse Golfer is at work . . .

THE ART OF COARSE ACTING

Michael Green

The Coarse Actor:
One who can remember his lines but not the order in which they come.
One who performs to sparse audiences in Church Halls amid lethal props.

The Coarse Actor's aim is to upstage the rest of the cast. His hope is to be dead by Act Two so that he can spend the rest of the time in the pub. His problems? Everyone else connected with the production.

I'VE LOST MY LITTLE WILLIE
Benny Green

The fat ladies, clumsy newlyweds, red-nosed drunks and downtrodden husbands of the comic postcard have been a colourful reflection of British humour, fashion and morals since the turn of the century. With calculated vulgarity and relentless innuendo, they present a defiantly optimistic worm's-eye view of the world.

Using much contemporary material in the form of photographs, news clippings and advertisements, Benny Green re-creates the salty, breezy milieu of the comic postcard in this affectionate tribute to the art of ribaldry.

SPORTING FEVER

Michael Parkinson

Ever known a centre-half who could break coconuts with his head? Or a bowler who got bitten by his own false teeth?

Sporting fever runs in the blood. Michael Parkinson inherited the disease from a cricket crazy grandfather who thought nothing of trudging thirty miles to see Yorkshire play, and it looks as if his own children have fallen prey to it.

Bill Shanklyn, Gary Sobers and Muhammed Ali number among the sporting personalities Parkinson has watched, met or played against. But so do some other less likely characters . . .

CRICKET MAD

Michael Parkinson

Michael Parkinson was born in a part of Yorkshire where it was perfectly normal to be cricket mad.

Since reaching a mature age and moving down south he has learned to curb his madness. Nowadays he stares out of train windows imagining he is Garfield Sobers rattling up a triple century.

He is not a member of the M.C.C. because he doesn't speak the language and moreover he has an irresistible desire to take off his shirt whenever he goes to Lords.

His favourite ground is Bramall Lane, his favourite flower is a white rose and his favourite cricketers are Yorkshiremen. He is renowned throughout cricket for the unbiased flavour of his writing.

Michael Parkinson

BEST: AN INTIMATE BIOGRAPHY

George Best – the greatest footballer of all time?

Certainly the most controversial. In his stormy, spectacular career, this wayward genius from the backstreets of Belfast attracted more praise – and more criticism – than any pop star or politician.

Now in one of the most intimate and revealing biographies ever published, Michael Parkinson tells the true, explosive story behind Best's dazzling success and tragic decline.

It's all here. The rows, the rivalries, the girls, the goals. With Best's own biting comments on the world he once ruled.